LISTEN, LITTLE MAN!

Love, work and knowledge are the well-springs of our
life. They should also govern it.

WILHELM REICH

My God!

WILHELM REICH

LISTEN, LITTLE MAN!

With illustrations by WILLIAM STEIG

Translated by THEODORE P. WOLFE

A Condor Book
SOUVENIR PRESS (EDUCATIONAL) & ACADEMIC LTD

Published in America by Farrar, Straus and Giroux, Inc.

First British edition published 1972
by Souvenir Press (Educational & Academic) Ltd.,
95 Mortimer Street, London, W.1

ISBN 0 285 62704 0 Hardback
ISBN 0 285 62705 9 Paperback

Printed in Great Britain by
Butler & Tanner Ltd., Frome and London

Ye specious worthies who scoff at me
Whence thrives your politics
As long as ye have ruled the world?
From dagger thrusts and murder!

Charles de Coster, ULENSPIEGEL

LISTEN, LITTLE MAN!

INTRODUCTION

LISTEN, LITTLE MAN! is a human and not a scientific document. It was written in the summer of 1945 for the Archives of the Orgone Institute without the intention of publishing it. It was the result of the inner storms and conflicts of a natural scientist and physician who watched, over decades, first naively, then with amazement and finally with horror, what the Little Man in the street *does to himself*; how he suffers and rebels, how he esteems his enemies and murders his friends; how, wherever he gains power as a "representative of the people," he misuses this power and makes it into something more cruel than the power which previously he had to suffer at the hands of individual sadists of the upper classes.

This "Talk" to the Little Man was the quiet answer to gossip and defamation. For decades, the emotional plague has tried again and again to kill orgone research (note well: not to prove it incorrect, but to kill it *by defamation*). Orgone research carries a very heavy responsibility for human life and health. This fact justifies the publication of this "Talk" as a historical document. It seemed necessary for the "man in the street" to learn what goes on in a scientific workshop and also to learn what he looks like to an experienced psychiatrist. He must learn to know reality which alone can counteract his disastrous craving for authority. He must be told clearly what *responsibility* he carries, whether he works, loves, hates or gossips. He must learn how he becomes a Fascist, be it the black or red variety. He who fights for the safeguarding of the living and the protection of our children must needs be against the red as well as the black Fascist. Not because today the red Fascist, like the black Fascist before him, has a murderous ideology, but because he turns lively and healthy children into

cripples, robots and moral idiots; because with him, the state comes
before right, the lie before truth, war before life; because the child,
and the safeguarding of the living in the child, remains our only
hope. There is only *one* loyalty for the educator and physician:
that to the living in the child and the patient. If this loyalty is
strictly adhered to, the great questions of "foreign politics" also find
their simple solution.

This "Talk" does not imply that one should make it the pattern
of one's existence. It describes storms in the emotional life of a
productive, happy individual. It does not want to convince or win
anybody. It pictures experience as a painting pictures a thunder-
storm. The reader is not asked to like it. He may read it or not.
It does not contain any intentions or programs. All it wants to do
is to win for the researcher and thinker the right to personal reaction
which one has never denied to the poet or philosopher. It is a protest
against the secret and unrecognized intention of the emotional
plague to shoot its poison arrows at the hardworking researcher,
from a safe ambush. It shows what the emotional plague is, how
it functions and retards progress. It also attests to the confidence
in the tremendous unmined treasures which lie in the depth of
"human nature," ready to be put in the service of fulfilling
human hopes.

The living, in its social and human interrelationships, is naively
kindly and thus, under prevailing conditions, endangered. It
assumes that the fellow human also follows the laws of the living
and is kindly, helpful and giving. As long as there is the emotional
plague, this natural basic attitude, that of the healthy child or the
primitive, becomes the greatest danger in the struggle for a rational
order of life. For the plague individual also ascribes to his fellow
beings the characteristics of his own thinking and acting. The
kindly individual believes that all people are kindly and act accord-
ingly. The plague individual believes that all people lie, swindle,

steal and crave power. Clearly, then, the living is at a disadvantage and in danger. Where it gives to the plague individual it is sucked dry and then derided or betrayed; and where it trusts it is cheated.

That's the way it has always been. It is time for the living to become hard where hardness is needed in the struggle for its safeguarding and development; in doing so, it will not lose its kindness if it sticks to the truth courageously. There is hope in the fact that, among millions of industrious, decent individuals there are always *only just a few* pestilential individuals who cause murderous mischief by appealing to the dark and dangerous impulses in the structure of the armored mass individual and lead them to organized political murder. There is only one antidote to the germs of the emotional plague in the mass individual: his own feeling of living life. The living does not ask for power but for its proper role in human life. It is based on the three pillars of love, work and knowledge.

He who has to protect the living against the emotional plague has to learn to use the right to free speech as we enjoy it in America at least as well for the good as the emotional plague misuses it for the bad. Granted equal right in the expression of opinion, the rational finally must win out. This is an important hope.

You are a "little, common man"

LISTEN, LITTLE MAN!

They call you "Little Man," "Common Man"; they say a new era has begun, the "Era of the Common Man." It isn't *you* who says so, Little Man. It is *they,* the Vice Presidents of great nations, promoted labor leaders, repentent sons of bourgeois families, statesmen and philosophers. They give you your future but don't ask about your past.

You are heir to a dreadful past. Your heritage is a burning diamond in your hand. That's what *I* tell you.

Every physician, shoemaker, mechanic or educator must know his shortcomings if he is to do his work and make his living. For some decades, you have begun to play a governing role on this earth. It is on your thinking and your actions that the future of humanity depends. But your teachers and masters do not tell you how you really think and are; nobody dares to voice the one criticism of you which could make you capable of governing your own fate. You are "free" only in one sense: free from education in governing your life yourself, free from self-criticism.

I have never heard you complain: "You promote me to be the future master of myself and my world, but you don't tell me how one is to be the master over oneself, and you don't tell me the mistakes in my thinking and my actions."

You let men in power assume power "for the Little Man." But you yourself remain silent. You give men in power or impotent people with evil intentions the power to represent you. Only too late do you realize that again and again you are being defrauded.

I understand you. For, many thousands of times, I have seen you naked, physically and psychically, without a mask, without a party card, without your "popularity." Naked like a newborn, naked like a Field Marshal in his underpants. You have complained and cried before me, have talked about your longings, and have disclosed your love and your grief. I know you and I understand you. I am going to tell you how you are, Little Man, for I honestly believe in your great future. There is no doubt, it belongs to you. So, first of all, have a look at yourself. See yourself as you really are. Listen to what none of your Führers and representatives dares tell you:

You are a *"little, common man."* Understand the double meaning of these words: "little," and "common."

Don't run. Have the courage to look at yourself!

"What right do you have to tell me things?" I can see this question in your apprehensive look. I hear this question from your impertinent mouth, Little Man. You are afraid to look at yourself, you are afraid of criticism, Little Man, just as you are afraid of the power they promise you. You would not know how to use this power. You dare not think that you ever might experience your self differently: free instead of cowed; open instead of tactical; loving openly instead of like a thief in the night. You despise yourself, Little Man. You say: "Who am I to have an opinion of my own, to determine my own life and to declare the world to be mine?" You are right: Who are you to make a claim to your life? I shall tell you who you are:

You are different from the really great man in only one thing: The great man, at one time, also was a very little man, but he developed *one* important ability: he learned to see where he was small in his thinking and actions. Under the pressure of some task which was dear to him he learned better and better to sense the threat that came from his smallness and pettiness. *The great man, then, knows when and in what he is a little man. The little man does not know that he is little, and he is afraid of knowing it.*

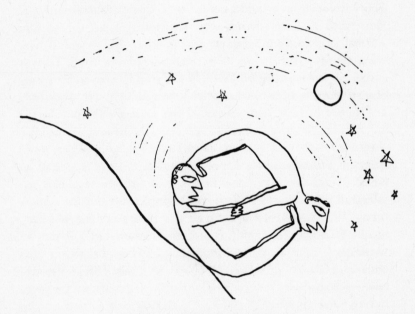

You are your own slave-driver

He covers up his smallness and narrowness with illusions of strength and greatness, of *others'* strength and greatness. He is proud of his great generals but not proud of himself. He admires the thought which he did *not* have and not the thought he *did* have. He believes in things all the more thoroughly the less he comprehends them, and does not believe in the correctness of those ideas which he comprehends most easily.

I shall begin with the little man in myself:

For twenty-five years, in the written and spoken word, I have advocated your *right to happiness in this world;* have accused you of your inability to take what belongs to you, to secure what you had gained in the bloody battles of the Paris and Vienna barricades, in the American emancipation or in the Russian revolution. Your Paris ended in Pétain and Laval, your Vienna in Hitler, your Russia in Stalin, and your America could end in the régime of a KKK. You knew better how to win your freedom than how to safeguard it for yourself and others. I have known this for a long time. What I could not understand was why, everytime you had fought your way laboriously out of one morass, you got into a worse one. Then, slowly and gropingly, I found what makes you a slave: YOU ARE YOUR OWN SLAVE-DRIVER. Nobody else — nobody except you yourself carries the responsibility for your slavery. Nobody else.

That is new to you, isn't it? Your liberators tell you that your suppressors are Wilhelm, Nikolaus, Pope Gregory the 28th, Morgan, Krupp or Ford. And your "liberators" are called Mussolini, Napoleon, Hitler, Stalin.

I tell you: *Only you yourself can be your liberator!*

This sentence makes me hesitate. I contend to be a fighter for pureness and truth. And now, when it is a matter of telling you the truth about yourself, I hesitate, because I am afraid of you and your attitude toward the truth. To say the truth about you is dangerous to life. The truth also is life-saving, but it becomes the loot of every gang. If that were not so, you would not be what you are and where you are.

Only you yourself can be your liberator!

My intellect tells me: Tell the truth, at any cost. The Little Man in me says: It is stupid to expose oneself to the Little Man, to put oneself at his mercy. The Little Man does not want to hear the truth about himself. He does not want the great responsibility which is his. He wants to remain a Little Man, or wants to become a little great man. He wants to become rich, or a party leader, or commander of the legion, or secretary of the society for the abolition of vice. But he does not want to assume the responsibility for his work, for food provision, housing, traffic, education, research, administration, or whatever it may be.

The Little Man in me says:

"You have become a great man, known in Germany, Austria, Scandinavia, England, America, Palestine, etc. The Communists fight you. The "saviors of cultural values" hate you. Your students love you. Your former patients admire you. Those afflicted with the emotional plague are after you. You have written 12 books and 150 articles about the misery of life, the misery of the Little Man. Your findings and theories are being taught at Universities; other great and lonely men say that you are a *very* great man. You are likened to the intellectual giants in the history of science. You have made the greatest discovery in centuries, for you have discovered the cosmic life energy and the laws of living functioning. You have made cancer comprehensible. You went from country to country, because you told the truth. Now, take it easy. Enjoy the fruits of your efforts, enjoy your fame. In a few years, your name will be heard everywhere. You have done enough. Now quit, and withdraw to your study to work on the functional law of nature!"

Thus speaks the Little Man in me who is afraid of you, the Little Man.

For a long time, I was in close contact with you because I knew your life from my own experience and because I wanted to help you. I kept up the contact because I saw that I really helped you and that you wanted my help, often enough with tears in your eyes. Very gradually, I began to see that you were willing to take my help but incapable of defending it. I did defend it and fought hard for you, in your stead. Then came your Führers and smashed my work. You remained silent and followed them. Now I kept up the contact in order to learn how one could help you without perishing, either as your Führer or your victim. The Little Man in me wanted to win you, to "save" you, he wanted to be regarded by you with the same reverence which you have for "higher mathematics" because you have not the faintest idea what it is all about. The less you understand, the more ready you are to give reverence. You know Hitler better than Nietzsche, Napoleon better than Pestalozzi. A king means more to you than a Sigmund Freud. The Little Man in me would like to win you as it is commonly done, with the means of the Führer. I become afraid of you when it is the Little Man in me who would "lead you to freedom." You

Anybody's slave

might discover yourself in me and me in you, might get scared and kill you in me. For this reason, I have ceased to be willing to die for your freedom to be anybody's slave.

I know you cannot understand what I just said: "Freedom to be anybody's slave" is not a simple matter.

In order no longer to be the slave of *one individual* master, in order to become *anybody's* slave, one first has to eliminate this one individual oppressor, say, the Tsar. This political murder one cannot commit without having high ideals of freedom and revolutionary motives. One then founds a revolutionary freedom party under the leadership of a truly great man, say, Jesus, Marx, Lincoln or Lenin. The truly great man takes your freedom deadly seriously. In order to establish it in a practical way, he has to surround himself with many little men, helpers and errand boys, because he cannot do the gigantic job by himself. Furthermore, you would not understand him, and would let him fall by the wayside, if he had not surrounded himself with little great persons. Surrounded by many little great persons, he conquers power for you, or a piece of truth, or a new, better belief. He writes gospels, freedom laws, etc., and counts on your help and seriousness. He pulls you out of your social morass. In order to keep together the many little great persons, in order not to lose your confidence, the truly great man has to sacrifice piece after piece of his greatness which he was able to attain only in the deepest intellectual loneliness, far from you and your everyday noise, and yet in close contact with your life. In order to be able to lead you he has to tolerate your transforming him into an inaccessible God. You would have no confidence in him if he had remained the simple man that he was, a man who, say, can love a woman even though he has no marriage certificate. In this way, *you* yourself produce your *new* master. Promoted to the role of new master, the great man loses his greatness because this greatness consisted in his straightforwardness, simplicity, courage and real contact with life. The little great persons, who derived their greatness from the great man, assume the high posts of finance, diplomacy, government, sciences and arts and you — remain where you were: *in the morass.* You continue to go in rags for the sake of a "Socialist future" or a "Third Reich." You continue to live in

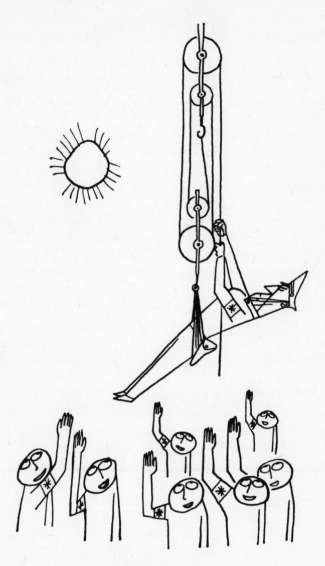

Little great man

dirt houses with straw roofs, the walls of which are covered with manure. But you are proud of your palace of culture. You are satisfied with the *illusion* that you govern — until the *next* war and the downfall of the *new* masters.

In distant nations, little men have industriously studied your craving for being anybody's slave and have thus learned how, with little intellectual effort, one can become a little great man. These little great men come from *your* ranks, not from palaces and mansions. They have hungered and suffered like you. They shorten the process of changing masters. They have learned that a hundred years of hard intellectual work on your freedom, of personal sacrifice for your happiness, even of sacrificing life for your freedom, was much too high a price for your new enslavement. What really great thinkers for freedom had elaborated and had suffered in 100 years could be destroyed in less than five years. The little men from your ranks, then, shorten the process: they do it more openly and more brutally. More than that, they tell you in so many words that you and your life, your family and your children, amount to *nothing,* that you are stupid and subservient, that one can do with you what one pleases. They do not promise you personal freedom, but *national* freedom. They do not promise you human self-confidence but respect for the state, not personal greatness, but national greatness. Since "personal freedom" and "personal greatness" are nothing to you but vague concepts, while "national freedom" and "the interests of the state" make your mouth water like a bone that of a dog, you loudly acclaim them. None of these little men pays the price for genuine freedom, as did Jesus, Karl Marx or Lincoln. They do not love you, they despise you, *since you despise yourself,* Little Man. They know you well, far better than a Rockefeller or the Tories know you. They know your worst weaknesses in a way in which only *you* should know them. They have sacrificed you to a symbol, and you carry them to power over yourself. Your masters have been elevated by you, yourself, and are nurtured by you, in spite of the fact — or, rather, because of the fact — that they dropped all masks. Indeed, they told you in so many words: "You are an inferior being without any responsibility, and you are going to remain so." And you call them "Saviors," "New Liberators," and yell: "Heil, Heil," and "Viva, viva!"

This is why I am afraid of you, Little Man, deadly afraid. For on you depends the fate of humanity. I am afraid of you because there is nothing you flee as much from as yourself. You are sick, very sick, Little Man. It is not your fault. But it is your responsibility to rid yourself of this sickness. You would have long since shaken off your oppressors had you not tolerated oppression and often actively supported it. No police force in the world would be powerful enough to suppress you if you had only a mite of self-respect in practical everyday living, if you knew, deep down, that without you life would not go on for even an hour. Did your "liberator" tell you that? No. He called you the "Proletarian of the World," but he did not tell you that you, and *only you,* are *responsible* for *your* life (instead of being responsible for the "honor of the fatherland").

You must come to realize that you made your little men your own oppressors, and that you made martyrs out of your truly great men; that you crucified and murdered them and let them starve; that you did not give a thought to them and their labors for you; that you have no idea to whom you owe whatever fulfilments there are in your life.

You say, "Before I trust you, I want to know your philosophy of life." When you hear my philosophy of life, you will run to your District Attorney, or to the "Committee against Un-American Activities," or to the FBI, the GPU or the "Yellow Press," or the

New Liberators

Ku-Klux Klan or the "Leaders of the Proletarians of the World," or, finally, you will simply run:

I am not a Red or a Black or a White or a Yellow.

I am not a Christian or a Jew or a Mohammedan, a Mormon, Polygamist, Homosexual, Anarchist or Boxer.

I embrace my wife because I love her and desire her and not because I happen to have a marriage certificate or because I am sexually starved.

I do not beat children, I do not fish and do not shoot deer or rabbits. But I am a good shot and like to hit the bull's-eye.

I do not play bridge and do not give parties in order to spread my theories. If my teachings are correct they will spread by themselves.

I do not submit my work to any health official unless he has mastered it better than I have. And *I* determine who has mastered the knowledge and the intricacies of my discovery.

I strictly observe every law when it makes sense, but I fight it when it is obsolete or senseless. (Don't run to the District Attorney, Little Man, for he does the same if he is a decent individual).

I want children and adolescents to experience their bodily happiness in love and to enjoy it without danger.

I do not believe that, in order to be religious in the good and genuine sense of the word, one has to ruin one's love life and has to become rigid and shrunken in body and soul.

I know that what you call "God" actually exists, but in a different way from what you think: as the primal cosmic energy in the universe, as your love in your body, as your honesty and your feeling of nature in you and around you.

I would show the door to anybody who, under whatever flimsy pretext, were to try to interfere with my medical and educational work with patient or child. In any open court, I would ask him some very simple and clear questions which he could not answer without being ashamed ever after. For I am a working man who knows what a man really is inside, who knows that he amounts to something, and who wants *work* to govern the world, and not opinions about work. I have my own opinion, and I can distinguish a lie from the truth which, every hour of the day, I use like a tool and which, after use, I keep clean.

I am very deeply afraid of you, Little Man. That has not always been so. I myself was a Little Man, among millions of Little Men. Then I became a natural scientist and a psychiatrist, and I learned to see how very sick you are and how dangerous you are in your sickness. I learned to see the fact that it is your own emotional sickness, and not an external power, which, every hour and every minute, suppresses you, even though there may be no external pressure. You would have overcome the tyrants long ago had you been alive inside and healthy. Your oppressors come from *your own* ranks as in the past they came from the upper strata of society. They are even littler than you are, Little Man. For it takes a good dose of littleness to know your misery from experience and then to use this knowledge to suppress you *still better, still harder.*

You have no sense organ for the truly great man. His way of being, his suffering, his longing, his raging, his fight for you are alien to you. You cannot understand that there are men and women who are incapable of suppressing or exploiting you, and who really want you to be free, real and honest. You do not like these men and women for they are alien to your being. They are simple and straight; to them, truth is what tactics is to you. They look through you, not with derision, but pained at the fate of humans; but you feel looked-through and sense danger. You acclaim them only, Little Man, when many other Little Men tell you that these great men are great. You are afraid of the great man, of his closeness to life and his love for life. The great man loves you simply as a *living animal,* as a *living being.* He does not want to see you suffer as you have suffered for thousands of years. He does not want to hear you babble as you have babbled for thousands of years. He does not want to see you as a beast of burden, because he loves life and would like to see it free from suffering and ignominy.

Your empty, babbling social "parties"

You drive really great men to the point where they despise you, where, pained by you and your pettinesses, they withdraw, where they avoid you and, worst of all, begin to *pity* you. If you, Little Man, happen to be a psychiatrist, say, a Lombroso, you stamp the great man as a kind of criminal, or a criminal who has failed to make good, or a psychotic. For the great man, unlike you, does not see the goal of life in amassing money, or in the socially proper marriage of his daughters, or in a political career, or in academic titles or the Nobel prize. For this reason, because he is not like you, you call him "genius" or "queer." He, on the other hand, is willing to state that he is no genius, but simply a living being. You call him "asocial" because he prefers the study, with his thoughts, or the laboratory, with his work, to your empty, babbling social "parties." You call him crazy because he spends his money for scientific research instead of buying bonds and stocks, as you do. You presume, Little Man, in your bottomless degeneration, to call the simple, straightforward man "abnormal," as compared with you, the proto-type of "normality," the *homo normalis.*" You measure him with your petty yardsticks and find that he does not meet the demands of your normality. You cannot see, Little Man, that it is you who drive him, who is full of love for you and readiness to help you, from social life because you have made it insufferable, be it in the tavern or in the palace. Who has made him into what he seems to be after many decades of heart-breaking suffering? It is *you,* with your irresponsibility, your narrowness, your false thinking, your "unshakeable axioms" that cannot survive 10 years of social development. Just think of all the things which you swore to be correct in as few years as have elapsed between the first and the second world war. How much of that have you honestly recog-nized to be erroneous, how much of it have you retracted? Absolutely nothing, Little Man. The truly great man thinks cau-tiously, but once he has gotten hold of an important idea, he thinks in long-range terms. It is you, Little Man, who makes a pariah out of the great man when his thought is *correct* and *lasting* and your thought is petty and ephemeral. In making him a pariah, you plant the dreadful seed of loneliness in him. Not the seed of loneliness which produces great deeds, but the seed of the fear of being misunderstood and maltreated by you. For you are "the

Instead, you asked yourself what your neighbor was going to say about it, or whether your honesty might cost you money

people," "public opinion," and "social conscience." Have you,
Little Man, ever honestly thought about the gigantic responsibility
involved in this? Have you ever — honestly — asked yourself
whether you think correctly or not, from the standpoint of long-
term social happenings, or of nature, or of great human deeds, say,
of a Jesus? No, you did not ask yourself whether your thinking
was erroneous. Instead, you asked yourself what your neighbor
was going to say about it, or whether your honesty might cost you
money. This, Little Man, and nothing else, is what you asked
yourself.

After thus having driven the great man into loneliness, you
forgot what you did to him. All you did was to utter other nonsense, to commit another little meanness, to administer another
deep hurt. You forget. But it is of the nature of the great men
not to forget, but also not to take revenge, but, instead, to try to
UNDERSTAND WHY YOU ACT SO SHABBILY. I know that this also is
alien to your thinking and feeling. But believe me: if you inflict
pain a hundred, a thousand, a million times, if you inflict wounds
that cannot heal — even though the next moment you no longer
know what you did — the great man suffers for your misdeeds in
your place, not because these misdeeds are great, but because they
are petty. He would like to know what moves you to do things
like these: to smear your marital partner because he or she has dis-
appointed you; to torture your child because he does not please a
vicious neighbor; to look with scorn on a kind person and to exploit him; *to take where you are given and to give where it is de-
manded of you, but never to give where you are given with love; to
give another kick to the fellow who is down or about to go down;*
to lie where truth is required, and always to persecute truth instead
of the lie. You are always on the side of the prosecutors, Little Man.

In order to gain your favor, Little Man, in order to gain your
useless friendship, the great man would have to adjust himself to

Secretly, you despise yourself, even when —
or particularly when — you make the greatest
display of your dignity

you, would have to talk the way you do, would have to adorn himself with your virtues. But if he had your virtues, your language and
your friendship, he would no longer be great and true and simple.
The proof: your friends who talked the way you wanted them to
talk have never been great men.

You do not believe that *your* friend could achieve something great.
Secretly, you despise yourself, even when — or particularly when —
you make the greatest display of your dignity; and since you despise
yourself you cannot respect him who is your friend. You cannot
believe that somebody who sat at the same table with you or lived
in the same house with you could achieve anything great. In your
proximity, Little Man, it is difficult to think. One can only think
about you, not *with* you. For you choke any great, sweeping thought.
As a mother you say to your child which explores its world: "That's
not a thing for children." As a professor of biology you say:
"That's nothing for decent students. What, doubt the theory of
the air germs?" As a teacher you say: "Children are to be seen and
not to be heard." As a wife you say: "Ha! Discovery! You with
your discovery! Why don't you go to the office like everybody else
and make a decent living?" But what is said in the newspaper
you believe, whether you understand it or not.

I tell you, Little Man: You have lost the feeling for the best
that is in you. You have strangled it, and you murder it where-
ever you detect it in others, in your children, your wife, your husband, your father and your mother. You are little and you want
to remain little.

You ask how I know all this? I'll tell you:

I have experienced you, I have experienced with you, I have experienced myself in you, I have, as a therapist, freed you from your
pettinesses, I have, as an educator, often led you to straightforwardness and openness. I know how you defend yourself against

"Air germs"

straightforwardness, I know the terror that strikes you when you are asked to follow your true, genuine being.

You are *not only* little, Little Man. I know you have your "big moments" in life, moments of "rapture" and "elation," of "soaring up." But you don't have the stamina to soar higher and higher, to let your elation carry you up and up. You are afraid of soaring, afraid of height and depth. Nietzsche has told you this much better, long ago. But he did not tell you *why* you are that way. He tried to make you into a superman, an "Uebermensch," in order to overcome the human in you. His Uebermensch became your "Führer Hitler." And you remained the "Untermensch."

But what is said in the newspapers you believe, whether you understand it or not

I want you to stop being an Untermensch and want you to become *yourself*. Yourself, instead of the newspaper you read or the poor opinion that you hear from your vicious neighbor. I know that you do not know what and how you really are deep down. In the depth, you are what a deer is, or your God, your poet or your wise man. But you believe that you are a member of the Legion, the bowling club or the Ku-Klux Klan. And since you believe this, you act as you do. This, too, you have been told by others: by Heinrich Mann in Germany as long as 25 years ago, and

You are afraid of soaring, afraid of height and depth

in America by Upton Sinclair, Dos Passos and others. But you didn't know of Mann or Sinclair. You know only the champion boxer and Al Capone. Faced with the choice between a library or a brawl, you will unquestionably choose the brawl.

You beg for happiness in life, but security is more important to you, even if it costs you your spine or your life. Since you have never learned to create happiness, to enjoy and protect it, you do not know the courage of the upright individual. You want to know, Little Man, how you are? You listen on the radio to the announcements of laxatives, dental creams and deodorants. But you fail to hear the music of propaganda. You fail to perceive the bottomless stupidity and the disgustingly bad taste of these things which are designed to catch *your* ear. Have you ever paid close attention to the jokes which a master of ceremonies makes about you in a night club? Jokes about you, about himself, about your whole small miserable world. Listen to your laxatives propaganda and you learn who and how you are.

Listen, Little Man: The misery of human existence becomes spotlighted by every one of these *petty* misdeeds. Every one of your pettinesses makes the hope for an improvement of your lot recede farther. This is cause for grieving, Little Man, deep, heart-breaking grieving. In order not to feel this grief, you make bad little jokes, and call it "folk humor." You hear the joke about yourself, and you laugh heartily with the others. You do not laugh because you make fun of yourself. You laugh at the Little Man, but you don't know that you laugh at yourself, that *one laughs at you.* Millions of Little Men do not know that one laughs at them. Why does one laugh at you, Little Man, so openly, so heartily, with such malicious joy, all through the centuries? Has it ever struck you as how ridiculous "the people" are presented in the movies? I will tell you why one laughs at you, *because I take you very, very seriously:*

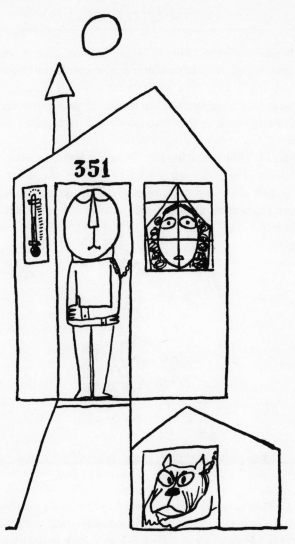

You beg for happiness, but security is more important to you

With the greatest consistency, your thinking always misses the truth, just as a playful sharpshooter is able consistently to hit right besides the bull's-eye. You don't think so? I'll show you. You could have long since become the master of your existence, if only your thinking were in the direction of the truth. But you think like this:

"It's all the fault of the Jews." "What's a Jew?" I ask. "People with Jewish blood," is your answer. "What's the difference between Jewish blood and other blood?" This question stumps you; you hesitate, become confused, and answer: "I mean the Jewish

You hear the joke about yourself, and you laugh heartily with the others

race." "What is race?" I ask. "Race? Why, that's simple: just as there is a German race, so there is a Jewish race." "What characterizes the Jewish race?" "Well, a Jew is dark-haired, has a long hooknose and sharp eyes. The Jews are avaricious and capitalistic." "Have you ever seen a Mediterranian Frenchman or Italian together with a Jew? Can you distinguish them?" "Well, not really."

"What, then, is a Jew? The blood picture shows no difference; he does not look different from a Frenchman or Italian. And have you ever seen *German* Jews?" "Sure, they look like Germans." "And what is a German?" "A German belongs to the Nordic Aryan race." "Are the Indians Aryans?" "Sure." "Are they Nordic?" "No." "Are they blond?" "No." "So you see, you don't know what is a German and what is a Jew." "But there are Jews." "Certainly there are Jews, just as there are Christians and Mohammedans." "I mean the Jewish religion." "Was Roosevelt a Dutchman?" "No." "Why do you call a descendant of David a Jew if you don't call Roosevelt a Dutchman?" "With the Jews it's different." "What's different?" "I don't know."

That's the way you drivel, Little Man. From your drivel you create armed formations and these slay 10 million people as "Jews," though you cannot even tell what a Jew is. That's why one laughs at you, why one avoids you when one has serious work to do, that's why you stick in the morass. When you say "Jew" you make yourself feel superior. You have to do that because you really feel miserable. And you feel miserable because you are precisely that which you murder in the alleged Jew. This is only a tiny bit of the truth about you, Little Man.

You feel your pettiness less when you say "Jew," arrogantly or contemptuously. It is only recently that I have found that out. You call somebody a "Jew" if he arouses too little or too much respect in you. You set out arbitrarily to determine who is a "Jew". But I do not concede this right to you, be you a little Aryan or a little Jew. Only I and nobody else in this world has the right to determine who I am. I am, biologically and culturally, a mongrel, and I am proud of being the intellectual and physical result of *all* classes and races and nations, proud of not being of a "pure race" like you, or belonging to a "pure class" like you, of not being chauvinistic like you, the little Fascist of all nations, races and

It took many million years to develop you from a jelly-fish to a terrestrian biped

classes. I hear that in Palestine you did not want a Jewish technician because he was not circumcised. I have nothing more in common with Jewish Fascists than with any others. Why, Little Jew, do you go back only to Sem, and not to the protoplasm? To me, the living begins in the plasmatic contraction, and not in a rabbi's office.

It took many million years to develop you from a jelly-fish to a terrestrian biped. Your biological aberration, in the form of rigidity, has lasted only six thousand years. It will take a hundred or five hundred or maybe five thousand years before you rediscover nature in you, before you find the jelly-fish in yourself again. I discovered the jelly-fish in you and described it to you in clear language. When you heard about it the first time, you called me a new genius. You will remember, it was in Scandinavia, at a time you were looking for a new Lenin. But I had more important things to do and declined this role. You have also proclaimed me to be a new Darwin, or Marx, or Pasteur, or Freud. I told you long ago that you too, would be able to talk and write like me, if you only would not always yell, Hail, Hail, Messiah! For this victorious yelling deadens your mind and paralyzes your creative nature.

Do you not persecute the "illegitimate mother" as an immoral being, Little Man? Don't you make a strict distinction between children "born in wedlock" who are "legitimate" and children "born out of wedlock" who are "illegitimate?" Oh you poor creature, you don't understand your own words: You venerate the child Christ. The child Christ was born by a mother who had no marriage certificate. Thus, without having any idea of it, you venerate in the child Christ your longing for sexual freedom, you Little Hen-pecked Man. You made the "illegitimately" born child Christ the Son of God, who did not know illegitimate children. But then, as the Apostle Paul, you began to persecute the children of true love and to give the children of true hatred the protection of your religious laws. You are a Miserable Little Man!

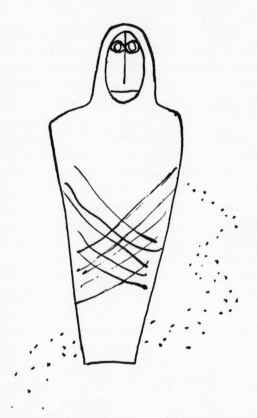

Your biological aberration, in the form of rigidity,
has lasted only six thousand years

You run your automobiles and trains over the bridges which the great Galileo invented. Do you know, Little Man, that the great Galileo had three children, without a marriage license? That you don't tell your school children. And, did you not torture Galileo for this reason also?

And do you know, Little Man in the "fatherland of Slavic Peoples," that your great Lenin, the greatest father of all proletarians of the world, abolished your compulsive marriage when he came to power? And do you know that he himself had lived with his wife without a marriage license? And did you not have, through your Führer of all Slavs, the old laws of compulsive marriage re-established, because you did not know that you should let Lenin's big deed live?

Of all this you know nothing at all, for what is truth to you, or history, or the fight for your freedom, and who are you, anyhow, to have an opinion of your own?

You have no inkling of the fact that it is your pornographic mind and your sexual irresponsibility which put you in the shackles of your marriage laws.

You feel yourself miserable and small, stinking, impotent, rigid, lifeless and empty. You have no woman, or if you have one, you only want to "lay" her in order to prove the "man" in you. You don't know what love is. You are constipated and take laxatives. You smell bad, your skin is clammy; you don't feel your child in your arm and so you treat it as a puppy that can be beaten up.

All your life you were bothered by your impotence. It invaded every thought of yours. It interfered with your work. Your wife left you because you were unable to give her love. You suffer from phobias, nervousness and palpitations. Your thoughts revolve around sexuality. Somebody tells you of sex-economy which understands you and would like to help you. It would like to make you live your sexuality *at night* so that during the day you would be *free* of sexual thoughts and capable of doing your work. It would like to see your wife happy in your arms instead of desperate. It would like to see your children rosy instead of pale, loving instead of cruel. But you, hearing of sex-economy, say: "Sex isn't everything. There are other important things in life." That's the way you are, Little Man.

Or you are a "Marxist," a "professional revolutionary," a would-be "Führer of the proletarians of the world." You want to free the world from its sufferings. The deceived masses run away from you, and you run after them, yelling: "Stop, stop, you proletarian masses! You just can't see yet that I am your liberator! Down with capitalism!" I talk to your masses, Little Revolutionary, I show them the misery of their small lives. They listen, full of enthusiasm and hope. They crowd into your organizations because they expect to find *me* there. But what do *you* do? You say: "Sexuality is a petit-bourgeois invention. It is the *economic* factors that count." And you read Van de Velde's book on love techniques.

When a great man set out to give your economic emancipation a scientific basis you let him starve. You killed the first inroad of truth against your deviation from the laws of life. When this first attempt of his was successful, you took over its administration and thus killed it a second time. The first time, the great man dissolved your organization. The second time, he had died in the meantime and could no longer do anything against you. You did not understand that he had found, in your *work,* the living power which creates values. You did not understand that his sociology wanted to protect your *society* against your *state.* You don't understand *anything at all!*

And even with your "economic factors" you don't get anywhere. A great, wise man worked himself to death to show you that you have to improve economic conditions if you want to enjoy your life; that hungry individuals are unable to further culture; that *all* con-

Proletarian General

ditions of life, without exception, belong here; that you have to emancipate yourself and your society from *all* tyranny. This true, great man made only one mistake when he tried to enlighten you: he believed in your capacity for emancipation. He believed you were capable of securing your freedom once you had conquered it. And he made another mistake: that of letting you, the proletarian, be a "dictator."

And what did you, Little Man, do with the wealth of knowledge and ideas coming from this great man? Of all of it, only *one* word kept ringing in your ears: *dictatorship!* Of all that a great mind and a big warm heart had poured out, one word remained: dictatorship. Everything else you threw overboard, freedom, clarity and truth, the solution of the problems of economic slavery, the method of thinking ahead; everything, but everything, went overboard. Only one word, which had been unhappily chosen though well meant, stuck with you: *dictatorship!*

From this small negligence of a great man you have built a giant system of lies, persecution, torture, goalers, hangmen, secret police, espionage and denunciation, uniforms, field marshals and medals — but everything else you have thrown overboard. Do you begin to understand a little better how you are, Little Man? Not yet? Well, let's try again: The "economic conditions" of your happiness in life and love you confused with "machinery"; the emancipation of human beings with the "greatness of the state"; the rising of millions with the parade of cannons; the liberation of love with the rape of every woman you could lay your hands on when you came to Germany; the elimination of poverty with the eradication of the poor, weak and helpless; infant care with the "breeding of patriots"; birth control with medals for "mothers with 10 children." Have you not suffered it yourself, this idea of yours of the mother with 10 children?

In other countries, too, the unfortunate little word, "dictatorship," rang in your ears. There, you put it into resplendent uniforms and you created from your midst the little, impotent, mystical and sadistic official who led you into the Third Reich and led 60 million of your kind to the grave. And you keep yelling, Hail, Hail, Hail!

That's the way you are, Little Man. But nobody dares tell you what you are like. For one is afraid of you and wants you to be *small,* Little Man.

You devour your happiness. Never have you enjoyed happiness in full freedom. That's why you greedily devour happiness, without taking responsibility for securing happiness. You were kept from learning to take care of your happiness, to nurture it as a gardener nurtures his flowers and the farmer his crops. The great searchers and poets and sages fled from you because they wanted to take care of their happiness. In your proximity, Little Man, it is easy to devour happiness but difficult to protect it.

You don't know what I am talking about, Little Man? I'll tell you: The discoverer works hard, for ten, twenty or thirty years, without let-up, on his science, or machine, or social idea. He has to carry the heavy burden of what is new all by himself. He has to suffer your stupidities, your erroneous little ideas and ideals, he has to comprehend and analyze them, and, finally, has to replace them by his deeds. In all this, you do not help him, Little Man. Not in the least. On the contrary. You don't come and say: "Listen, fellow, I see how hard you work. I also realize that you work on *my* machine, *my* child, *my* wife, *my* friend, *my* house, *my* fields, in order to improve things. For a long time, I have suffered from this and that, but I could not help myself. Now, can I help you to help me?" No, Little Man, you never come to your helper to help. You play cards, or you yell yourself hoarse at a prize-fight, or you slave away dully in an office or a mine. But never do you come to help your helper. You know why? Because the discoverer, to begin with, has nothing to offer but *thoughts*. No profit, no higher

You devour your happiness

wages, no union contract, no Christmas bonus and no easy way of living. All he has to give out are cares, and you don't want any cares, you have more than enough already.

But if you just stayed away, not offering or giving help, the discoverer would not feel unhappy about you. After all, he does not think and worry and discover "for" you. He does all this because his living functioning drives him to do it. The taking care of you and the pitying you he leaves to the party leaders and the churchmen. What he would like to see is that you finally become capable of *taking care of yourself*.

But you are not content with not helping; you disrupt and spit. When the discoverer finally, after long and hard work, has come to understand why you are incapable of giving your wife happiness in love, you come and say that *he* is a sexual swine. You have no inkling of the fact that you say this because you have to keep down the sexual swine in yourself and that *that is why* you are incapable of love. Or, when the discoverer has just found out why people die of cancer, *en masse,* and if you, Little Man, happen to be a Professor of Cancer Pathology, with a steady salary, you say that the discoverer is a faker; or that he does not understand anything about the air germs; or that he spends or gets too much money for his research; or you ask whether he is a Jew, or a foreigner; or you insist that you have a right to examine him, in order to find out whether he is qualified to work on "your" cancer problem, the problem you cannot solve; or you prefer to see many, many cancer patients die rather than to admit that *he* has found what *you* so badly need if you are to save your patients. To you, your professorial dignity, or your bank account, or your connection with the radium industry means more than truth and learning. And that's why you are small and miserable, Little Man.

That is, not only do you not help, but you disturb maliciously work that is done *for you* or in your stead. Do you understand now why happiness escapes you? *It wants to be worked for and wants to be earned.* But you only want to devour happiness; that's why it escapes you; it does not want to be devoured by you.

In the course of time, the discoverer succeeds in convincing many people that his discovery has practical value, that, say, it makes it possible to treat certain diseases, or to lift a weight, or to blast rocks, or to penetrate matter with rays so that the inside becomes visible. You do not believe it until you read it in the newspapers, for you don't trust your own senses. You respect the one who despises you, and you despise yourself; that is why you cannot trust your own senses. But when the discovery is written up in the newspapers, then you come, not walking, but running. You declare the discoverer to be a "genius," the same man whom yesterday you called a faker, a sexual swine, a charlatan or a dangerous man who undermined public morals. Now you call him a "genius." You don't know what a genius is, as you don't know what a "Jew" is, or "truth" or "happiness?" I'll tell you, Little Man, as Jack London has told you in his Martin Eden. I know you have read it thousands of times, but you have not *grasped* it: *"Genius" is the trade mark you put on your products when you put them on sale.* If the discoverer (who only yesterday was a sexual swine" or "crazy") is a "genius," then it is easier for *you* to devour the happiness which *he* has put in the world. For now there come *very many* little men and cry, in unison with you, "Genius, genius." And people come in droves and eat your products from your hand. If you are a physician, you will have many more patients; you can help them much better than previously and can make much more money. "Well," you say, Little Man, "nothing bad about that." No, there is certainly nothing bad about earning money with honest and good work. But it *is bad* not to give back anything to the discovery, not to take care of it, but *only* to exploit it. And that is precisely what you are doing. You do nothing to further the development of the discovery.

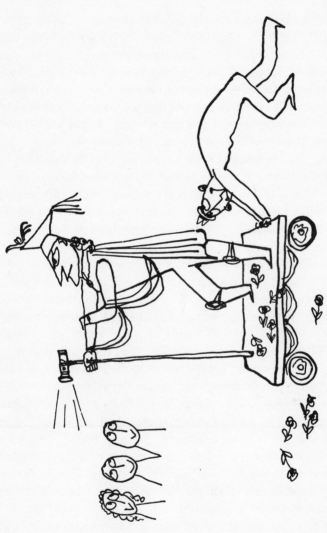

You want a wing-clipped and dressed-up genius whom, without blushing, you can trium-phantly parade through the streets of your town

You take it over mechanically, greedily, stupidly. You do not see its possibilities or its limitations. As to the possibilities, you don't have the vision, and as to the limitations, you don't recognize them and go beyond them. If, as a physician or bacteriologist, you know typhoid or cholera to be infectious diseases, you look for a micro-organism in the cancer disease and thus stultify decades of research. Once a great man showed you that machines follow certain laws; then you build machines for killing, and you take the living to be a machine also. In this, you made a mistake not for three decades, but for three *centuries;* erroneous concepts became inextricably anchored in hundreds of thousands of scientific workers; more, life itself was severely damaged; for from this point on — because of your dignity, or your professorship, your religion, your bank account or your character armor — you persecuted, slandered and otherwise damaged anyone who really was on the track of the living function.

True enough, you want to have "geniuses" and you are willing to pay them homage. But you want a *good* genius, one with moderation and decorum, one without folly, in brief, a *seemly, measured and adjusted* genius, not an unruly, untamed genius which breaks down all your barriers and limitations. You want a limited, wing-clipped and dressed-up genius whom, without blushing, you can triumphantly parade through the streets of your towns.

That's the way you are, Little Man. You are good at scooping up and ladling in, but *you cannot create*. And that's why you are what you are, all your life in a boring office or at the designing board or in the marital straight-jacket or a teacher who hates children. You have no development and no chance for a new thought, because you have always only taken, only ladled in what somebody else has presented to you on a silver platter.

You don't see why this is so, why it cannot be otherwise? I'll tell you, Little Man, for I have come to know you as an animal become rigid when you came to me with your inner emptiness or your impotence or your mental disorder. You can only ladle in and only take, and cannot create and cannot give, because your basic bodily attitude is that of *holding back* and of *spite;* because panic strikes you when the primordial movement of LOVE and of GIVING stirs in you. This is why you are *afraid of giving.* Your taking, basically, has only *one* meaning: You are forced continuously to gorge yourself with money, with happiness, with knowledge, because you feel yourself to be empty, starved, unhappy, not genuinely knowing nor desirous of knowledge. For the same reason you keep running away from the truth, Little Man: it might release the love reflex in you. It would inevitably show you what I, inadequately, am trying to show you here. And that you do not want, Little Man. You only want to be a consumer and a patriot.

"Listen to that! He denies patriotism, the bulwark of the state and of its germ, the family! Something has to be done about it!"

That's the way you yell, Little Man, when one reminds you of your psychic constipation. You don't want to listen to it or know it. You want to yell, Hurrah! All right, but why don't you let me tell you quietly why you are incapable of happiness? I see fear in your eyes; this question seems to concern you deeply. You are for "religious tolerance." You want to be free to like your own religion. Well and good. But you want more than that: you want *your* religion to be the only one. You are tolerant as to your religion, but not tolerant as to others. You become rabid when somebody, instead of a personal God, adores nature and tries to understand it. You want a marital partner to sue the other, to accuse him or her of immorality or brutality when they no longer can live together. Divorce on the basis of mutual agreement you do not recognize, you little descendant of great rebels. For you are frightened by your own lascivity. You want the truth in a mirror, where you can't grasp it. Your chauvinism derives from your bodily rigidity, your psychic constipation, Little Man. I don't say this derisively, but because I am your friend; even though you slay your friends when they tell you the truth. Take a look at your patriots: They do not walk; they march. They do not hate the enemy; instead, they have "hereditary enemies" whom they exchange every 10 years or so, making them hereditary friends, and back into hereditary enemies. They do not sing songs; they yell martial airs. They do not embrace their women; they "lay" them and "do" so and so many "numbers" a night. There is nothing you can undertake against my truth, Little Man. All you can do is to slay me, as you have slain so many others of your true friends: Jesus, Rathenau, Karl

This is why you steal your happiness like a thief in the night

Liebknecht, Lincoln, and many others. In Germany, you used to call it "putting down." In the long run, it has put *you* down, by the millions. But you continue to be a patriot.

You long for love, you love your work and make a living from it, and your work lives on my knowledge and that of others. Love, work and knowledge know no fatherlands, no custom barriers, no uniforms. They are international and comprise all humanity. But you want to be a little patriot, because you are afraid of genuine love, afraid of your responsibility for your own work, afraid of knowledge. This is why you can only exploit the love, work and knowledge of others but can never create yourself. This is why you steal your happiness like a thief in the night; this is why you cannot see happiness in others without getting green with envy.

"Stop thief! He is a foreigner, an immigrant. But I am a German, an American, a Dane, a Norwegian!"

Ah, stop it, Little Man! You are and remain the eternal immigrant and emigrant. You have entered this world quite accidentally and will silently leave it again. You yell because you are afraid. You feel your body go rigid and gradually dry up. That's why you

You yell because you are afraid

are afraid and call for your police. But your police has no power over my truth either. Even your policeman comes to me, complaining about his wife and his sick children. When he dons his uniform he hides the man in himself; but he cannot hide from me; I have seen him naked, too.

"Is he registered with the police? Are his papers in order? Has he paid his taxes? Investigate him. He is a danger to the state and the honor of the nation!"

Yes, Little Man, I have always been properly registered, my papers are in order and I have always paid my taxes. What you worry about is not the state or the honor of the nation. You tremble with fear lest I disclose your nature in public as I have seen it in my medical office. That's why you look for ways of convicting me of a political crime which would put me in jail for years. I know you, Little Man. If you happen to be an Assistant District Attorney, you are not interested in *protecting* the law or the citizen; what you need is a whacking "case" in order to advance more quickly to the post of District Attorney. That's what the little Assistant District Attorneys want. They did the same thing with Socrates. But you never learn from history. You murdered Socrates, and because you still do not know that you did, you continue to remain in the morass. You accused him of undermining your good morals. He still undermines them, poor Little Man. You murdered his body but you could not murder his mind. You continue to murder, in the interest of "order"; but you murder in a cowardly, cunning way. You could not look me in the eyes when you accuse me publicly of immorality. For you know which one of us is immoral, lascivious and pornographic. Somebody once said that among his numerous acquaintances there was only one he had never heard tell a dirty joke; I was the one. Little Man, whether you be a District Attorney, a judge or a chief of police, I know your little dirty jokes, and I know the source from which they stem. So, better keep quiet. Well, you might succeed in showing that my income tax payment was 100 dollars short; or that I drove across a state line with a woman; or that I talked nicely with a child in the street. But it is in *your* mouth that each of these three sentences assumes its special timbre, the slippery, equivocal, mean sound of vile action. And

"Longing"

since you know of nothing else, you think that I am like you. No, Little Man, I am not like you and never was like you in these things. It does not matter whether you believe it or not. True, you have a revolver and I have knowledge. The roles are divided.

You ruin your own existence, Little Man, in the following manner:

In 1924, I suggested a scientific study of the human character. You were enthusiastic.

In 1928, our work achieved its first tangible results. You were enthusiastic and called me a "spiritus rector."

In 1933, I was to publish these results in book form, in your publishing house. Hitler had just come to power. I had learned to understand the fact that Hitler came to power because your character is armored. You refused to publish the book in your publishing house, the book which showed you how you produce a Hitler.

The book appeared nonetheless, and you continued to be enthusiastic. But you tried to kill it by silence, for your "President" had declared himself against it. He had also advised mothers to suppress the genital excitations of infants by means of holding the breath.

For 12 years, then, you kept silent about the book which aroused your enthusiasm. In 1946, it was reissued. You acclaimed it as a "classic." You still are enthusiastic about my book.

22 long, anxious, eventful years have passed since I began to teach you that what is important is not individual treatment but the *prevention* of mental disorders. For 22 long years I taught you that people get into this or that frenzy, or remain stuck in this or that lamentation, because their minds and bodies have become rigid and because they can neither give love nor enjoy it. This, because their bodies, unlike that of other animals, cannot contract and expand in the love act.

22 years after I had first said this, you now say to your friends that what is important is not individual treatment but the prevention

of mental disorders. And you act *again* as you have acted for thousands of years: you mention the big goal without saying how it could be reached. *You fail to mention the love life of the masses of people.* You want to "prevent mental disorders." That you can say; it is harmless and dignified. But you want to do it *without tackling the prevailing sexual misery.* You do not even mention it; that is not allowed. And as a physician, you remain stuck in the morass.

What would you think of a technician who reveals the technique of flying but fails to disclose the secrets of the motor and the propeller? That's the way you act, the technician of psychotherapy. You are a coward. You want to pick the cherries out of my pie, but you don't want the thorns of my roses. Don't you, too, crack dirty jokes about me, "the prophet of the better orgasm?" Don't you, little psychiatrist? Have you never heard the plaints of young brides whose bodies had been violated by impotent husbands? Or the anguish of adolescents who burst with unfulfilled love? Is your security still more important to you than your patient? How long are you going to continue putting your dignity in the place of your medical task? How long are you going to overlook the fact that your tactics cost the life of millions?

You set security before the truth. When you hear of the orgone which I discovered you do not ask: "What can it do? How can it cure patients?" No, you ask: "Is he licensed to practice medicine in the state of Maine?" You don't know that your little licenses can do no more than disturb my work a little; they cannot prevent it. You don't know that I have worth everywhere on this earth, as the discoverer of your emotional plague and of your life energy; that nobody can examine me who does not know more than I.

Now, as to *your freedom giddiness.* Nobody, Little Man, has ever asked you why you have not been able to get freedom for yourself, or why, if you did, you immediately surrendered it to some new master.

"Listen to that! He dares to doubt the revolutionary upsurge of the proletarians of the world, he dares to doubt democracy! Down with the counter-revolutionary! Down!"

Down with him!

Don't get excited, little Führer of all democrats and all proletarians of the world. I believe that your *real* freedom of the future depends more on the answer to this *one* question than on tens of thousands of resolutions of your Party Congresses.

"Down with him! He sullies the honor of the nation and of the avant-guard of the revolutionary proletariat! Down! Against the wall!"

Your yelling "Viva!" and "Down!" is not going to get you one step closer to your goal, Little Man. You have been believing that your freedom is secured when you "put people against the wall."

For once, *put yourself in front of a mirror!*

"Down, down!"

Stop a minute, Little Man. I do not want to belittle you, I only want to show you why up to now you have not been able to get freedom or to hold it. Aren't you interested in that at all?

"Down, down, down!"

All right, I shall be brief: I shall tell you how the Little Man in you behaves if you happen to find yourself in a situation of freedom. Let's assume you are a student at an Institute which stands for sexual health in children and adolescents. You are enthusiastic over the "splendid idea" and want to participate in the fight. This is what happened in my house:

My students sat at their microscopes, observing earth bions. You were sitting in the orgone accumulator, naked. I called to you to take part in the observations. Whereupon you jumped out of the accumulator naked, amidst the girls and women, exposing yourself. I reprimanded you immediately, but you did not see why I should have. I, on my part, could not understand why you did not see. Later, in an extended discussion, you admitted that that had been precisely your concept of freedom in an Institute which advocates sexual health. You soon found out that you had the deepest *contempt* for the Institute and its basic idea, and that was why you had behaved indecently.

Another example, to show how again and again you gamble away your freedom. You know, and I know, and everybody knows, that you go around in a perpetual state of sexual starvation; that you look greedily at every member of the other sex; that you talk with your friends about love in terms of dirty jokes; in brief, that you have a dirty, *pornographic* phantasy. One night, I heard you and your friends walk along the street, yelling in unison: "We want women! We want women!"

Concerned with your future, I built up organizations in which

you might learn better to understand your misery in life and to do
something about it. You and your friends came to these meetings
in droves. Why was that, Little Man? At first I thought it was
because of an honest, burning interest in improving your life. Only
much later did I recognize what really motivated you. You thought
that here was a new kind of brothel, where one could get a girl
easily and without shelling out money. Realizing that, I smashed
these organizations which were designed to help you with your
life. Not because I think it is bad to find a girl in a meeting of
such an organization, but because you approached it with a filthy
mind. That's why these organizations were destroyed, and, again,
you remained stuck in the morass. . . You wanted to say something?

"The proletariat has been spoiled by the bourgeoisie. The Führers
of the proletariat will help. They are going to clean up the mess
with a mailed fist. Apart from that, the sexual problem of the
proletariat is going to solve itself."

I know what you mean, Little Man. That's exactly what they
did in your fatherland of proletarians: to let the sexual problem
solve itself. The result was shown in Berlin, when the proletarian
soldiers raped women all night long. You know that as a fact.
Your champions of the "revolutionary honor," "the soldiers of
the proletarians of the world" have sullied you for centuries to
come. You say such things happened "only in the war?" Then
I'm going to tell you another true story:

A would-be Führer, full of enthusiasm for the dictatorship of the
proletariat, was also enthusiastic about sex-economy. He came to
me and said: "You are wonderful. Karl Marx has shown the people
how they can be free *economically*. You have shown the people
how they can be free *sexually*: you have told them: 'Go out and
fuck as much as you like'." In your head, everything becomes a
perversion. What I call the loving embrace becomes, in your life, a
pornographic act.

Berlin nights

You don't even know what I'm talking about, Little Man. This is why, again and again, you sink back into the morass.

If you, Little Woman, by mere chance, without any special qualifications, have become a teacher, simply because you did not have children of your own, you do untold damage. Your job is to handle and educate children. In education, if one takes it seriously, this means correctly to manage the children's sexuality. *In order correctly to handle the children's sexuality, one must oneself have experienced what love is.* But you are fat, awkward and unattractive. That alone is enough to make you hate every charming, alive body with deep and bitter hatred. What I am blaming you for is not that you are fat and unattractive; not that you have never enjoyed love (no healthy man would give it to you); nor that you do not understand love in the children. What I am blaming you for is that you make a virtue out of your unattractiveness and your incapacity for love, and that, with your bitter hatred, you strangle the love in the children, if you happen to work in a "progressive school." This is a crime, ugly Little Woman. The harmfulness of your existence consists in your alienating the affection of healthy children from their healthy fathers; in your considering the healthy love of a child a pathological symptom. It consists in your being barrel-shaped, your going around like a barrel, your thinking like a barrel, your educating like a barrel; in your not modestly retiring to a small corner of life, but, instead, trying to impose upon this life your barrel shape, your falseness, and your bitter hatred hidden behind your false smile.

And, Little Man, because you let such women handle your healthy children, let them drip their bitterness and their poison into healthy souls, are you what you are, live as you live, think as you think, and is the world as it is.

Again, this is what you are like, Little Man: You came to me in order to learn what I, in hard work, had found out and had fought

You think like a barrel, you educate like a barrel, you try to im-pose upon this life your barrel shape, your falseness, and your bitter hatred hidden behind your false smile

for. Without me, you would have become a small, unknown general practitioner in some small town or village. I made you great by giving you my knowledge and my therapeutic technique. I taught you to see the manner in which freedom is suppressed, every minute of the day, and how lack of freedom is nurtured. Then you assume a responsible position as the exponent of my work in some other country. You are free in the full sense of the word. I trust your honesty. But you feel inwardly dependent on me because you are unable to develop much out of yourself. You need me in order to drink knowledge from me, to get self-confidence, vision into the future, and, more than anything else, *development*. All this I give to you gladly, Little Man. I ask nothing in return. But then you declare that I "raped" you. You become fresh, in the belief of being free. But to confuse impudence with freedom has always been the sign of the slave. Pointing to your freedom, you refuse to send reports about your work. You feel yourself free — free from co-operation and responsibility. And that's why, Little Man, you are what you are, and that's why the world is what it is.

Do you know, Little Man, how an eagle would feel if he were hatching chickens' eggs? At first the eagle thinks that he will hatch little eagles whom he is going to bring up to be big eagles. But what comes out of the eggs is always nothing but little chicks. Desperate, the eagle keeps hoping that the chicks will turn into eagles after all. But no, at the end they are nothing but cackling hens. When the eagle found out this, he had a hard time suppressing his impulse to eat up all the chicks and cackling hens. What kept him from doing so was a small hope. The hope, namely, that among the many cackling chicks there might be, one day, a little eagle capable of growing up into a big eagle, capable like himself, to look from his lofty perch into the far distance, in order to detect new worlds, new thoughts and new forms of living. It was only this small hope that kept the sad, lonely eagle from eating up all the

The eagle's chicks

cackling chicks and hens. They did not see that they were being
hatched by an eagle. They did not see that they lived on a high,
steep rock, far above the damp, dark valleys. They did not look
into the distance like the lonely eagle. They only gobbled and
gobbled and gobbled whatever the eagle brought home to them.
They let him warm them under his powerful wings when it rained
and stormed outside, when he withstood the storm without any
protection. Or, if things got tougher, they threw sharp little rocks
at him from ambush, in order to hit and hurt him. When he
realized this maliciousness his first impulse was to tear them to
shreds. But he thought about it and began to pity them. Sometime,
he hoped, there would be, there would have to be, among the many
cackling, gobbling and short-sighted chickens, a little eagle capable
of becoming like himself.

The lonely eagle, to this day, has not given up this hope. And so
he continues to hatch little chickens.

You do not want to become an eagle, Little Man, and that is
why you get eaten by the vultures. You are afraid of the eagles,
and so you live together in great herds, and are being eaten up in
big herds. For some of your chickens have hatched the eggs of
vultures. And the vultures have become your Führers against the
eagles, the eagles who wanted to lead you into farther, better distances. The vultures taught you to eat carrion and to be content
with just a few grains of wheat. In addition, they taught you to yell,
"Hail, Hail, Great Vulture!" Now you starve and die, in great
masses, and you still are afraid of the eagles who hatch your chickens.

All these things, Little Man, you have built on sand: your house,
your life, your culture and civilization, your science and technic,
your love and your education of children. You don't know it, you
don't want to know it, and you slay the great man who tells it to
you. You come, in great distress, asking again and again the same
questions:

"My child is stubborn, he smashes everything, he cries out in night-mares, he can't concentrate on his schoolwork, he suffers from constipation, he is pale, he is cruel. What should I do? Help me!"

Or: "My wife is frigid, she doesn't give me any love. She tortures me, she has hysterical fits, she runs around with a dozen men. What shall I do? Tell me!"

Or: "A new, even more dreadful war has broken out, and this after we had fought the war to end all wars. What should we do?"

Or: "The civilization of which I am so proud is collapsing, as a result of this inflation. Millions of people have nothing to eat, they starve, they murder, steal, deteriorate, and give up all hope. What should we do?"

"What should I do?" "What should one do?" This is your eternal question through the centuries.

The fate of great achievement, born from a way of living which sets truth before security, is this: to be greedily devoured by you and to be shit out again by you.

A great many great, courageous and lonely men have told you long since what you should do. Again and again, you have twisted their teachings, torn them apart and destroyed them. Again and again, you tackled them from the *wrong* end, made the small error instead of the great truth the guiding line of your life, in Christianity, in the teaching of socialism, in the teaching of the sovereignty of the people, in absolutely everything you touched, Little Man. Why do you do this, you ask? I don't believe that your question is seriously meant. You will feel murderous when you hear the truth:

You built your house on sand and you did all this because you are incapable of feeling life in yourself, because you kill love in your child even before it is born; because you cannot tolerate any alive expression, any free, natural movement. Because you cannot toler-ate it, you get scared and ask: "What is Mr. Jones, and what is Judge Smith going to say?"

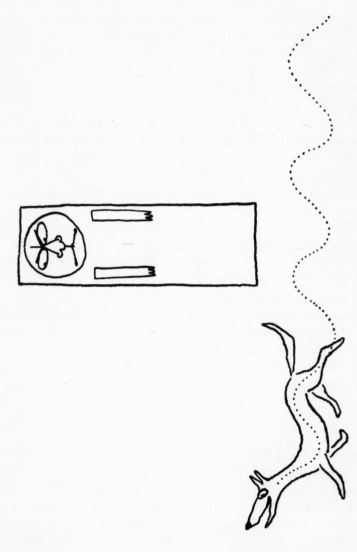

You cannot tolerate any alive expression, any free, natural movement

You are cowardly in your thinking, Little Man, because real thinking is accompanied by bodily feelings, and you are afraid of your body. Many great men have told you: Go back to your origin — listen to your inner voice — follow your true feelings — cherish love. But you were deaf to what they said, for you had lost your ear for such words. They were lost in vast deserts, and the lonely criers perish in your dreadful desert emptiness, Little Man.

You had the choice between Nietzsche's elevation to the Uebermensch and Hitler's degradation into the Untermensch. You cried, Heil!, and chose the Untermensch.

You had the choice between the genuinely democratic constitution of Lenin and the dictatorship of Stalin. You chose the dictatorship of Stalin.

You had the choice between Freud's elucidation of the sexual core of your emotional disease and his theory of cultural adaptation. You chose his cultural philosophy which did not give you a leg to stand on, and forgot about the theory of sex.

You had the choice between the majestic simplicity of Jesus and the celibacy of Paul for his priests and life-long compulsive marriage for yourself. You chose celibacy and compulsive marriage, forgetting about Jesus's simple mother who bore her child Christ out of love only.

You had the choice between Marx's realization of the productivity of your living working power, which alone produces the value of goods, on the one hand, and the idea of the state on the other. You forgot about the living in your work, and chose the idea of the state.

During the French Revolution, you had the choice between the cruel Robespierre and the great Danton. You chose cruelty and sent greatness and kindness to the gallows.

In Germany, you had the choice between Goering and Himmler on the one hand and Liebknecht, Landau and Mühsam on the other. You made Himmler your chief of police, and you murdered your true friends. You had the choice between Julius Streicher and Walter Rathenau. You murdered Rathenau.

You had the choice between Lodge and Wilson. You murdered Wilson.

You had the choice between the cruel Inquisition and the truth of Galileo. You tortured to death the great Galileo, from whose discoveries you are profiting, by submitting him to utter humiliation. In this 20th century, you have again brought to flower the methods of the Inquisition.

You had the choice between an understanding of mental disease and shock therapy. You chose shock therapy, in order not to have to realize the gigantic dimensions of your own misery, in order to continue to remain blind where only open, clear eyes can help.

You have the choice between ignorance of the cancer cell and my disclosure of its secrets which could and will save millions of human lives. You keep repeating the same stupidities about cancer in periodicals and newspapers and keep silent about the knowledge which might save your child, your wife or your mother.

You starve and die by the million, but you fight the Mohammedans about the sacredness of cows, Little Indian Man. You go in rags, Little Italian and Little Slav of Trieste, but you have no other worry than whether Trieste is "Italian" or "Slavic." I thought Trieste was a harbor for ships from all over the world.

You hang the Hitlerites *after* they have murdered millions of people. What were you thinking *before* they had killed millions? Aren't dozens of corpses enough to make you think? Does it take millions of corpses to stir your humanity?

Each one of these pettinesses elucidates the gigantic misery of the animal, man. You say: "Why do you take all this so damn seriously? Do you feel responsible for all and every evil?" In saying this, you condemn yourself. If you, Little Man out of millions,

Send your politicians and diplomats packing

carried even a mite of your responsibility, the world would look different, and your great friends would not die of your pettinesses.

It is because you don't take any responsibility that your house stands on sand. The ceiling collapses over you, but you have a "proletarian" or a "national" honor. The floor collapses under you, but going down you still yell, "Heil, great Führer, long live German, Russian, Jewish honor!" The waterpipes break, your child is drowning; but you continue to advocate "discipline and order" which you teach your child with beatings. Your wife lies in bed with pneumonia, but you, Little Man, consider what is a foundation of rock the product of a "Jewish phantasy."

You come running to me and ask me: "My good, dear, great Doctor! What should I do? My house is collapsing, the wind blows through it, my child and my wife are sick, and so am I. What should I do?" The answer is: Build your house on rock. The rock is your own nature which you kill in yourself, the bodily love of your child, the dream of love of your wife, your own dream of life at the age of 16. Exchange your illusions for a bit of truth. Send your politicians and diplomats packing. Forget about your neighbor and listen to what is in you; your neighbor too will be grateful. Tell your fellows in work all over the world that you are willing to work for *life* only, and no longer for death. Instead of running to the executions of your hangmen and hanged, *create a law for the protection of human life and goods*. Such a law will be part of the rock under your house. Protect the love of your small children against the attacks of lascivious, ungratified women and men. Prosecute the gossiping spinster; expose her publicly or put her in a reform school instead of the adolescents who long for love. Do no longer try to outdo your exploiter in exploitation when you are in a position to guide work. Throw away your striped pants and your high hat and don't ask for a license to embrace your wife. Make contact with people in other countries, for they are like you,

Coney Island

in their good qualities and bad. Let your child grow up as nature
(or "God") has made it. Don't try to improve nature. Try, instead, to understand and protect it. Go to a library instead of a
prize-fight, to foreign countries instead of Coney Island. And,
most important, THINK CORRECTLY, listen to your inner voice which
nudges you gently. You have your life in your own hand. Do
not entrust it to anybody else, least of all to the Führers you elected.
BE YOURSELF! Many great men have told you so.

"Listen to this reactionary petit-bourgeois individualist! He does
not know the inexorable course of history. "Know thyself," he says.
What bourgeois nonsense! The revolutionary proletariat of the
world, led by its beloved Führer, the father of all peoples, of all
the Russians, of all the Slavs, will free the people! Down with the
individualists and anarchists!"

And long live the Fathers of all peoples and all Slavs, Little
Man! Listen, Little Man, I have some serious predictions to make:

You are taking over the rule of the world, and it makes you
tremble with fear. For centuries to come, you will murder your
friends and will hail as your masters the Führers of all peoples,
proletarians and all the Russians. Day after day, week after week,
decade after decade, you will praise one master after the other; and
at the same time you will not hear the plaints of your babies, the
misery of your adolescents, the longings of your men and women,
or, if you hear them, you will call them bourgeois individualism.
Through the centuries, you will shed blood where life should be
protected, and will believe that you will achieve freedom with the
help of the hangman; thus, you will find yourself again and again in
the same morass. Through the centuries, you will follow the brag-
garts and will be deaf and blind when LIFE, YOUR LIFE, calls to you.
For you are afraid of life, Little Man, deadly afraid. You will
murder it, in the belief of doing it for the sake of "socialism," or
"the state," or "national honor," or "the glory of God." There is

You are afraid of life

one thing you don't know nor want to know: *That you yourself create all your misery, hour after hour, day after day; that you do not understand your children, that you break their spines before they have had a chance really to develop them; that you steal love; that you are avaricious and crazy for power; that you keep a dog in order* also *to be a "master."* Through the centuries you will miss your way, until you and your like will die the mass death of the general social misery; until the awfulness of your existence will spark in you a first, weak glimmer of insight into yourself. Then, gradually and gropingly, you will learn to look for your friend, the man of love, work and knowledge, will learn to understand and respect him. Then you will begin to understand that the library is more important for your life than the prize-fight; a thoughtful walk in the woods better than parading; healing better than killing; healthy self-confidence better than national consciousness, and modesty better than patriotic and other yelling.

You think the goal justifies the means, even the vile means. You are wrong: *The goal is in the path on which you arrive at it. Every step of today is your life of tomorrow.* No great goal can be reached by vile means. That you have proven in every social revolution. The vileness or inhumanity of the path to the goal makes you vile or inhuman, and the goal unattainable.

"But how, then, shall I reach my goal of Christian love, of socialism, of the American constitution?" Your Christian love, your socialism, your American constitution lie in what you do every day, what you think every hour, in how you embrace your mate and how you experience your child, in how you look at your work as YOUR SOCIAL RESPONSIBILITY, in how you avoid becoming like the suppressor of your life.

But you, Little Man, misuse the freedoms given you in the constitution in order to *overthrow* it, instead of making it take root in everyday life.

I saw you as a German refugee misuse Swedish hospitality. At that time, you were a would-be Führer of all the suppressed people on earth. You remember the Swedish institution of smörgasbord? Many foods and delicacies are spread out, and it is left to the guest what and how much he will take. To you, this institution was new and alien; you could not understand how one can trust human decency. You told me with malicious joy how you did not eat all day in order to gorge yourself on the free food in the evening.

"I have starved as a child," you say. I know, Little Man, for I have seen you starve, and I know what hunger is. But you don't know that you perpetuate the hunger of your children a million times when you steal smörgasbord, you would-be savior of all the hungry. There are certain things one just does not do: such as stealing silver spoons, or the woman, or smörgasbord in a hospitable home. After the German catastrophe, I found you half-starved in a park. You told me that the "Red Help" of your party had refused to help you because you could not show your party membership, having lost your party book. Your Führers of all the hungry distinguish red, white and black hungry people. But we know only one starving organism. This is the way you are in *small* matters.

And this is the way you are in *big* matters:

You set out to abolish the exploitation of the capitalist era and the disdain for human life, and to get recognition of your rights. For there was, a hundred years ago, exploitation and contempt for human life, and thanklessness. But there also was respect for great achievements, and loyalty for the giver of great things, and recognition of gifts. And what have you done, Little Man?

Wherever you enthroned your own little Führers, the exploitation of your strength is more acute than a hundred years ago, the disdain for your life is more brutal, and there is no recognition of your rights at all. And where you are still trying to enthrone your own Führers, every respect for achievement has disappeared and been replaced by stealing the fruits of the hard work done by your great friends. You don't know what recognition of a gift is, for you think you would no longer be a free American or Russian or Chinese, if you were to respect and recognize things. *What you set out to destroy flourishes more vigorously than ever; and what you should safeguard and protect like your own life you have destroyed.* Loyalty you consider "sentimentality" or a "petty-bourgeois habit," respect for achievement slavish boot-licking. You do not see that you are boot-licking where you should be irreverent and that you are ungrateful where you should be loyal.

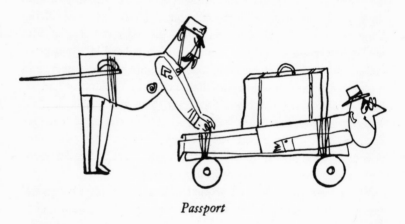

Passport

You stand on your head and you believe yourself dancing into the realm of freedom. You will wake up from your nightmare, Little Man, finding yourself helplessly lying on the ground. *For you steal where you are being given, and you give where you are being robbed.* You confuse the right to free speech and to criticism with irresponsible talk and poor jokes. You want to criticize but you don't want to be criticized, and for this reason you get torn apart. You always want to attack without exposing yourself to attack. That's why you always shoot from ambush.

"Police! Police! Is his passport in order? Is he really a Doctor of Medicine? His name is not in WHO IS WHO, and the Medical Association fights him."

The police won't help here, Little Man. They can catch thieves and can regulate traffic, but they cannot get freedom for you. You have destroyed your freedom yourself, and go on destroying it, with an inexorable consistency. Before the first "World War," there were no passports in international travel; you could travel wherever you wished. The war for "freedom and peace" brought the passport controls, and they stuck to you like lice. When you wanted to travel some 300 kilometers in Europe, you first had to ask for permission in the consulates of some 10 different nations. And so it still is, years after the termination of the second war to end all wars. And so it will remain after the third and nth war to end all wars.

"Listen! He sullies my patriotism, the honor and the glory of the nation!"

Oh, be quiet, Little Man. There are two kinds of tones: the howling of a storm about mountain tops, and — your fart. You are a fart, and you believe to smell of violets. I cure your neurotic misery and you ask whether I am in WHO IS WHO? I understand your cancer, and your little Commissioner of Health prohibits my experimenting with mice. I taught your physicians to understand you medically, and your Medical Association denounces me to the police. You are mentally ill, and they administer electric shocks to you, just as in the Middle Ages they used the chain or the whip.

Be quiet, Dear Little Man. Your life is all too miserable. I do not want to save you, but I shall finish my talk to you, even if you should come around in a white nightshirt and a mask, with a rope in your cruel, bloody hand, to hang me. You cannot hang me,

Little Man, without stringing up yourself. For I represent your life, your feeling of the world, your humanity, your love and your joy in creating. No, you cannot murder me, Little Man. Once I was afraid of you, just as before I had believed in you too much. But I have gone beyond you, and now I see you in the perspective of thousands of years, forwards and backwards in time. I want you to lose your fear of yourself. I want you to live more happily and more decently. I want you to have a body which is alive instead of rigid, I want you to love your children instead of hating them, to make your wife happy instead of "maritally" torturing her. I am your physician, and since you inhabit this planet, I am a planetary physician; I am not a German, or a Jew, or a Christian, or an Italian, I am a citizen of the *earth*. For you, on the other hand, there exist only angelical Americans and beastly Japanese.

"Grab him! Examine him! Does he have a license to practice medicine? Proclaim a Royal decree that he cannot practice without the consent of the king of our free country! He does experiments about my pleasure function! Jail him! Throw him out of the country!"

I have myself acquired the permission to engage in my activities. Nobody can give it to me. I have founded a new science which finally understands your life. You will avail yourself of it in ten, a hundred or a thousand years as in the past you have gobbled up other teachings when you were at the end of your rope. Your Minister of Health has no power over me, Little Man. He would have influence only if he had the courage to know my truth. But he does not have this courage. So he goes back to his country and tells people that I am interned in an American mental hospital, and he appoints as Inspector General of Hospitals a mediocre man who, in an attempt to deny the pleasure function, had falsified experiments. I, on the other hand, write this talk to you, Little Man. Do you want more proof of the impotence of your powers that be?

Your authorities, Commissioners of Health and Professors could not enforce their prohibitions against understanding your cancer. I did my dissecting and microscopic work against their explicit prohibition. Their travels to England and France to undermine my work were to no avail. They remained stuck where they had always been, in *pathology*. I, on the other hand, have saved your life more than once, Little Man.

"When I bring my Führers of all proletarians to power in Germany, we shall put him against the wall! He spoils our proletarian youth! He contends that the proletariat suffers from incapacity for love just as does the bourgeoisie! He makes brothels out of our youth organizations. He contends that I am an animal! He destroys my class consciousness!"

Yes, I destroy your ideals which cost you your good sense and your head, Little Man. You want to see your great eternal hope in the mirror only, where you can't grasp it. *But only the truth in your own fist will make you the master of this earth.*

"Throw him out of the country! He undermines quiet and order. He is a spy of my eternal enemies. He has bought a house with money from Moscow (or is it Berlin?)!"

You don't understand, Little Man. A little old woman was afraid of mice. She was my neighbor and knew that I kept experimental mice in my basement. She was afraid the mice might crawl under her skirt and between her legs. She would not have this fear if she had ever enjoyed love. It was in these mice that I learned to understand your cancerous putrefaction, Little Man. You happened to be my landlord, and the poor little woman asked you to evict me. And you, with all your courage, your wealth of ideals and ethics, evicted me. I had to buy a house in order to continue to examine the mice for you, undisturbed by you and your cowardice. After this, what did you do, Little Man? As an ambitious little District Attorney you wanted to use the famous dangerous man to further your career. You said I was a German, or, again, a Russian spy. You had me jailed. But it was worth it, seeing you sitting there at my hearing, blushing all over. I felt sorry for you, little servant of the State, so miserable were you. And your secret agents did not speak at all well of you when they searched my house for "espionage material."

Later, I met you again, this time in the person of a small Judge from the Bronx, with the unfulfilled ambition for a seat on a higher bench. You accused me of having books of Lenin and Trotzky in my library. You did not know, Little Man, what a library is for. I told you that I also had Hitler and Buddha and Jesus and Goethe and Napoleon and Casanova in my library. For, so I told you, in order to understand the emotional plague, one had to know it intimately from all sides. This was new to you, Little Judge.

"Jail him! He is a Fascist! He despises the people!"

You are not "the people," Little Judge. *You* despise the people, for you do not administer *their* rights, but, instead, further *your* career. This, too, you have been told by many great men; but, of course you never read them. I have respect for the people when I expose myself to the great danger of telling them the truth. I might play bridge with you and joke with you. But I do not sit at the same table with you. For you are a poor advocate of the Bill of Rights.

"He is a Trotzkyite! Jail him! He incites the people, the Red Dog!"

I do not incite the people, but your self-confidence, your humanity, and you can't stand it. For what you want is to get votes and advance in position, you want to be Judge of the Superior Court or Führer of all proletarians. Your justice and your Führer mentality is the rope around the neck of the world. What did you do with Wilson, this great, warm person? To you, the Judge from

Cancer Research

the Bronx, he was a "dreamer"; to you, the would-be Führer of all proletarians, he was an "exploiter of the people." You murdered him, Little Man, with your indolence, your empty talk, your fear of your own hope.

You almost murdered me, too, Little Man.

Do you remember my laboratory, ten years ago? You were technical Assistant. You had been out of work and had been recommended to me, as an outstanding Socialist, member of a government party. You received a good salary and were free in the full sense of the word. I included you in all deliberations, for I believed in you and your "mission." Do you remember what happened? You went crazy with freedom. For days, I saw you walk around with your pipe in your mouth, doing nothing. I did not understand why you did not work. When I came into the laboratory in the morning, you waited provocatively for me to greet you first. I like to greet people first, Little Man. But if one *waits* for me to do so, I get angry because I am, in *your* sense, your "Senior" and "Boss." I let you misuse your freedom for a few days, and then had a talk with you. With tears in your eyes, you admitted that you did not know what to do with this new kind of régime. You were not used to freedom. In your previous position, you had not been allowed to smoke in the presence of your chief, you were supposed only to speak when spoken to, you would-be Führer of all proletarians. But now, when you had *genuine* freedom, you behaved impertinently and provocatively. I understood you and did not fire you. Then you left and told some abstinent court psychiatrist about my experiments. *You* were the secret informer, one of the hypocrites and plotters who instigated the newspaper campaign against me. That's the way you are, Little Man, when you enjoy freedom. Contrary to your intentions, your campaign set my work ahead by ten years.

So I take leave of you, Little Man. I am no longer going to serve you, and I do not want to be slowly tortured to death by my concern for you. You cannot follow me into the far distances into which I move. You would be terrified if you had an inkling of what awaits you in the future. For you are taking over the rule of the world. My lonely reaches are a part of your future. But as yet I do not want you as a traveling companion. As a traveling companion, you are harmless only in the tavern, not where I am going.

"Down with him! He derides the civilization which I, the Man In The Street, have built up. I am a free man in a free democracy. Hurrah!"

You are nothing, Little Man, *nothing at all.* It is not you who has built up this civilization, but a very few of your decent masters. You haven't any idea what you are building when you are on a building job. And when somebody tells you to take responsibility for the building you call him a "traitor to the proletariat" and run to the Father of all Proletarians who does *not* tell you so.

Nor are you free, Little Man. You have no idea what freedom is. You would not know how to live in freedom. Who has carried the emotional plague to victory in Europe? You, Little Man. And in America? Think of Wilson.

"Listen, he accuses *me,* the Little Man! Who am I, what power have I, to influence the President of the United States? I do my duty, I do what my boss tells me, and I do not meddle in high politics."

And when you drag thousands of men, women and children to the gas chambers, you also just do what you are told to do, is that it, Little Man? You are so harmless that you don't even know what's going on. You are only a poor devil who has nothing to say, who has no opinion of his own, and who are you anyhow to meddle in politics? I know, I have heard it often enough. But I ask you: Why don't you do your duty when somebody tells you that you are responsible for your work, or tells you not to beat your children, or not to follow any dictators? Where is your duty, your harmless obedience, then? No, Little Man, you do not listen when truth speaks, you listen only when noises are being made. And then you

You put your General on a pedestal in order to be able *to respect him*

yell, Heil! You are cowardly and cruel, without any sense of your true duty, that of being *human* and of safeguarding *humanity*. You are poor at imitating the man who knows and so good at imitating the robber. Your films, radio programs and "comic books" are full of murder.

You will have to drag yourself and your pettinesses through the

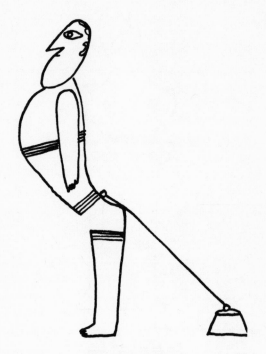

"*Homo normalis*"

centuries before you can become your own master. I separate from you in order better to serve your future. For in the distance you cannot slay me, and you have more respect for my work when it is at a distance. *You have contempt for that which is close to you.* You put your General or Field Marshal on a pedestal in order *to be able* to respect him, even though he is contemptible. That's why the great man has kept at a distance from you ever since the world has been writing its history.

"He is a megalomaniac! He's gone crazy, absolutely crazy!"

I know, Little Man, you are quick with the diagnosis of craziness when you meet a truth you don't like. And you feel yourself as the "homo normalis." You have locked up the crazy people, and the normal people manage this world. Who, then, is to blame for all the misery? Not you, of course, you only do your duty, and who are you to have an opinion of your own? I know, you don't have to repeat it. It isn't you that matters, Little Man. But when I think of your newborn children, of how you torture them in order to make them into "normal" human beings after your image, then I am tempted to come close to you again, in order to prevent your crime. But I also know that you have taken care to protect yourself well by your institution of a Department of Education.

I want to take you for a walk through this world, Little Man, and show you what you are and what you were, in the present and in the past, in Vienna, London and Berlin, as the "bearer of the popular will," as the member of some creed. You can find yourself everywhere, and you could recognize yourself, whether you are a Frenchman, a German or a Hottentot, if you had the courage to look at yourself.

"Listen! He offends my honor! He sullies my mission!"

I don't do any such thing, Little Man. I shall be very glad if you set me right, if you *prove* that you are able to look at yourself and to recognize yourself. You have to give proof the same way a con-

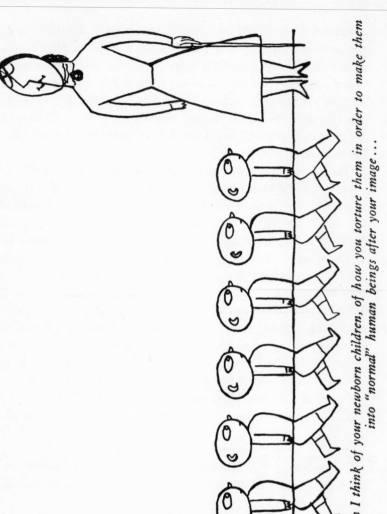

When I think of your newborn children, of how you torture them in order to make them into "normal" human beings after your image . . .

tractor who builds a house has to. The house must be there and it must be livable. The contractor has no right to yell, "He offends my honor," when I show him that he only talks about "the mission of housing construction" instead of actually building houses. In the same way, you have to *prove* that you are the bearer of the future of humanity. You can no longer hide, a coward, behind your "honor of the nation" or of the "proletariat." For you have disclosed too much of yourself, Little Man.

As I say, I am taking leave of you. It took many years and it cost many painful sleepless nights to do so. Your would-be Führers of all proletarians are not so complicated. Today they are your Führers and tomorrow they do hack writing for a little paper. They change their convictions as one changes shirts. I do not. I continue to care for you and your fate. But since you are incapable of respecting anyone who is close to you, I have to put some distance between us. Your great-grandchild will be the heir of my labors. I wait for him to enjoy my fruits as I have been waiting for thirty years for you to do so. You, instead, kept yelling, "Down with capitalism" or, "Down with the American Constitution!"

Follow me, Little Man, I want to show you some snapshots of yourself. Don't run. It is ugly, but salutary, and not so terribly dangerous.

About a hundred years ago you learned to parrot the physicists who built machines and said there was no soul. Then came a great man and showed you your soul, only he did not know the connection between your soul and your body. You said: "Ridiculous! 'Psychoanalysis!' Charlatanry! You can analyze urine, but you cannot analyze the psyche." You said this because in medicine you knew nothing but urine analysis. The fight for your mind lasted some forty years. I know this hard fight, because I, too, fought it for you. One day you discovered that one can make a lot of money with the sick human mind. All one has to do is to let a patient come daily for an hour over a period of some years and have him pay a certain fee for every hour.

Then, and not until then, did you begin to believe in the existence of the mind. In the meantime, knowledge of your body has quietly grown. I found that your mind is a function of your life energy, that, in other words, there is a unity between body and mind. I followed this track, and I found that you reach out with your life energy when you feel well and loving, and that you retract it to the center of the body when you are afraid. For fifteen years you kept silent about these discoveries. But I continued on the same track and found that this life energy, which I termed "orgone," is also found in the atmosphere, outside of your body. I succeeded in seeing it in the dark and to devise apparatus which magnified it and made it light up. While you were playing at cards or were torturing your wife and ruining your child, I sat in a darkroom, many hours a day, over two long years, to make sure that I had discovered your life energy. Gradually, I learned to demonstrate it to other people, and I found that they saw the same thing I saw.

If you are a doctor who believes that the mind is a secretion of the endocrine glands, you tell one of my cured patients that my therapeutic success was the result of "suggestion." If you suffer from obsessive doubts and fear of the dark, you say about the phenomena which you just observed that they were due to "suggestion" and that you feel as if in a spiritualist session. That's the way you are, Little Man. You blabber just as hopelessly about the "soul" in 1945 as you denied its existence in 1920. You have remained the same Little Man. In 1984, you will just as unconcernedly make a lot of money with the orgone, and will just as unconcernedly sully, doubt, defame, kill by silence and ruin another truth as you did with the discovery of the mind and with that of the cosmic energy. And you remain the "critical" Little Man who yells, Heil here and Heil there. You remember what you said about the

discovery that the earth does not stand still but rotates and moves
in the space? Your answer was the silly joke that now the glasses
would fall off a waiter's tray. That was a few centuries back and,
of course, you have forgotten, Little Man. All you know of Newton
is that "he saw an apple fall from a tree," and all you know of
Rousseau is that he "wanted to go back to nature." What you
learned from Darwin is only the "survival of the fittest," but not
your origin from the apes. Of Goethe's Faust, that you like to
quote so freely, you have understood as much as a cat understands
of mathematics. You are stupid and vain, empty and apish, Little
Man. You always know how to evade the essential and to take
over what is erroneous. Your Napoleon, this little man with the
gold braid, of whom nothing remained but compulsory military
training, is displayed in your bookshops in large golden letters, but
my Kepler, who foresaw your cosmic origin, cannot be found in any
bookstore. That's why you don't get out of the morass, Little Man.
That's why I have to tell you off when you believe that I have worked
and worried for twenty years and sacrificed a fortune in order to
"suggest" the existence of the cosmic orgone energy to you. No,
Little Man, by making all this sacrifice, I have really learned to cure
the plague in your body. You don't believe that. For I heard you
say in Norway that "if anybody spends that much money for his
experiments he must be literally crazy." I understood this: you
judge by yourself. *You can only take, you cannot give.* That's
why is is inconceivable to you that someone could have his joy in life
in giving, just as it is inconceivable to you that one could be together with a member of the other sex without immediately want-
ing to "lay."

I could respect you if you were *big* in stealing your happiness.
But you are a little, cowardly thief. You are clever but, being
psychically constipated, you are unable to create. Thus, you steal
a bone and crawl into a hole to chew it up, as Freud told you once.

You congregate around the voluntary giver, the cheerful spender, and suck him dry. You are the sucker and, perversely, you call *him* the sucker. *You gorge yourself with his knowledge, his happiness, his greatness, but you cannot digest what you have swallowed.* You shit it out again right away, and it stinks frightfully. Or, in order to maintain your dignity after having committed the theft, you sully your giver, call him crazy or a charlatan or a seducer of children.

Oh, there we are: "Seducer of children." Do you remember, Little Man (you were then the President of a scientific society) how you spread the rumor that I had my children witness the sexual act? This was after I had published my first article on the genital rights of infants. And the other time (you then happened to be the temporary President of some "cultural association" in Berlin) when you spread the rumor that I took adolescent girls for automobile rides into the woods and seduced them? I have never seduced adolescent girls, Little Man. That's *your* dirty phantasy, not mine, I love my girl or my wife; I am not like you who are incapable of loving your wife and therefore would like to seduce little girls in the woods.

And you, adolescent girl, don't you dream of your film star? Don't you take his picture to bed with you? Don't you approach him and seduce him, pretending to be over 18 years old? And then? Don't you go to court and accuse him of rape? He is acquitted, or found guilty, and your grandmothers kiss the hands of the great film star.

You wanted to sleep with the film star, but you did not have the courage to take the responsibility. So you accuse *him,* poor, violated girl. Or you poor, raped woman who experienced more sexual pleasure with her chauffeur than with her husband. Did you not seduce your colored chauffeur, who had kept his sexuality more nearly healthy, little white woman? And didn't you then accuse him of rape, poor helpless creature, the victim of an "inferior race?"

No, of course, you were pure, and white, your ancestors came over on the Mayflower, you are a "Daughter of This or That Revolution," a Northerner or a Southerner whose grandfather grew rich by dragging African Negroes to America in chains. How harmless, how pure, how white, how little desirous of the Negro you are, poor little woman. You miserable coward, descendent of a sick race of slave-hunters, of a cruel Cortez who lured thousands of trusting Aztecs into a trap in order to shoot them from ambush.

Daughter of This or That Revolution

You poor daughters of this or that revolution. What have you grasped about the emancipation? What of the strivings of the American revolutionaries, what of Lincoln who freed the slaves for you whom you then turned over to the "free market of competition"? Look in the mirror, daughters of revolutions. You will recognize there the "Daughters of the *Russian* Revolution," you harmless, chaste girls.

If you had been able to give love to a man a single time, the life of many a Negro, Jew or worker would have been saved. Just as

you kill your life in your children so you kill in the Negroes your
inkling of love, your frivolous pornographic phantasy of lust. I
know you, you girls and women of the rich. What abysmal vileness you breed in your rigid genitals! No, you daughter of this or
that revolution, I have no intention of becoming an LL.D. or a
Comissar. That I leave to your stiff creatures in robes and uniforms.
I love the birds and deer and chipmunks who are close to the
Negroes. I mean the Negroes from the jungle, not the ones from
Harlem, in stiff collars and zoot suits. I don't mean the fat Negro
women with ear rings whose inhibited pleasure turned into the fat
of their hips. I mean the svelte, soft bodies of the girls of the South
Sea whom you, the sexual swine of this or that Army, "lay"; girls
who do not know that you take their pure love as you would in a
Denver brothel.

No, daughter, you long for the living which as yet has not understood that it is exploited and despised. But your time has come.
You have ceased to function as the German racial virgin. You
continue to live as the Russian class virgin or as the Universal
daughter of the Revolution. In 500 or 1000 years, when healthy
boys and girls will enjoy and protect love, nothing will be left of
you but a ridiculous memory.

Did you not refuse your auditoriums to Marian Anderson, this
voice of the living, Little, Cancerous Woman? Her name will sing
into the centuries when no trace will be left of you. I ask myself
whether Marian Anderson also *thinks* into the centuries, or whether
she, too, prohibits her child's love. I don't know; the living swings
in big and small leaps. It is satisfied with life itself. It does not live
in you, Little Cancerous Woman.

You have spread the fairy tale, and your Little Man has swallowed
it, line, hook and sinker, that *you* are "THE SOCIETY," Little Woman.
You are not. True, you announce every day, in the Jewish and
Christian papers, that and when your daughter will embrace a man;

but this does not interest any serious individual. "Society" is *I* and the *carpenter* and the *gardener* and the *teacher* and the *physician* and the *factory worker*. That is society, and not you, the little, cancerous, stiff, mask-faced woman. You are not life, you are its distortion. But I understand why you withdrew into your wealthy fortress. It was the only thing you could do, in the face of the pettiness of the carpenters and the gardeners and the physicians, teachers and factory workers. In the framework of this plague, it was your wisest deed. But your smallness and pettiness is in your bones, with your constipation, your rheumatism, your mask, your denial of life. You are unhappy, poor little woman, because your sons go to ruin, your daughters become whores, your husbands dry up, and your life putrifies, and with it your tissues. You can't tell me any stories, Little Daughter of the Revolution; I have seen you naked.

You are cowardly and always have been. You had the happiness of humanity in your hands, and you have gambled it away. You have born Presidents, and have endowed them with pettiness. They get photographed pinning medals on people, they smile eternally and do not dare to call a spade a spade, Little Daughter of the Revolution! You had the world in your hands, and at the end you dropped your atom bombs on Hiroshima and Nagasaki; your son, I mean, dropped them. You dropped your tombstone, Little Cancerous Woman. With this one bomb, you bombed your whole class, your whole race, into the silent grave for ever. For you did not have the humanity to warn the men, women and children in Hiroshima and Nagasaki. You did not manage the greatness to be human. For this reason, you will silently disappear like a stone in the sea. It does not matter what you now think or say, you Little Woman who produced idiotic generals. Five hundred years from now, one will laugh and marvel at you. That one does not do so already is part and parcel of the misery of the world.

I know what you are going to say, Little Woman. All appear-

ances are in your favor; "defense of the country," etc. I've heard
that way back in the Old Austria. Have you ever heard a Viennese
coach driver yell, "Hurrah, mein Kaiser"? No? Well, you only
have to listen to yourself; it is the same music. No, Little Woman,
I am not afraid of you; there is nothing you can do to me. True,
your son-in-law is the Assistant District Attorney, or your nephew is
the Assistant Tax Collector. You invite him to tea and drop a few
words about me. He wants to become District Attorney or Chief
Tax Collector, and looks for a victim of "law and order." I know
how these things are done. But that sort of thing is not going to
save your neck, Little Woman. My truth is stronger than you.

"He is a one-sided fanatic! Don't I have *any* function in society?"

I have only shown you in what way you are *small* and *vile*, Little
Man and Little Woman. I have not even mentioned yet your use-
fulness and importance. Do you think I would give you a talk
fraught with danger to life if you were not important? Your
pettinesses and meannesses seem all the more terrible if seen in the
light of your importance and giant responsibility. They say you are
stupid. I say you are clever but *cowardly*. They say you are the
offal of human society. I say you are its seed. They say culture
needs slaves. I say no culture can be built with slaves. This dreadful 20th century has made ridiculous every cultural theory evolved
since Plato. *Human culture does not even exist yet, Little Man!*
We are only just beginning to comprehend the dreadful deviation
and pathological degeneration of the animal, man. This "Talk to
the Little Man" or any other decent writing of today is to the
culture of 1000 or 5000 years hence as was the first wheel of thousands of years ago to the Diesel locomotive of today.

You always think in too short terms, Little Man, just from break-
fast to lunch. You must learn to think back in terms of centuries
and forward in terms of thousands of years. You have to learn to
think in the terms of living life, in terms of *your* development from

the first plasmatic flake to the animal man which walks erect but cannot yet think straight. You have no memory even for things which happened 10 or 20 years ago, and so you keep repeating the same stupidities you said 2000 years ago. More than that, you cling to your stupidities, such as your "race," "class," "nation," religious compulsion and suppression of love as a louse clings to a fur. You do not dare see how deeply you stick in the morass of your misery. Every once in a while, you stick your head out of the morass to yell, Heil! The croaking of a frog in a marsh is closer to life.

Every once in a while you stick your head out of the morass to yell, Heil!

"Why don't you get me out of the morass? Why don't you take part in my party councils, my parliaments, my diplomatic conferences? You are a traitor! You have fought for me and suffered and sacrificed. Now you insult me!"

I cannot get you out of your morass. The only one who can do that is you yourself. I have never taken part in your councils and conferences because the cry there is always, "Down with the essential!" and "Let's talk about the non-essential." True, for 25 years I have fought for you, have sacrificed my professional security and the warmth of my family for you; I have given a good deal of money to your organizations, have taken part in your parades and hunger marches. True, I have given you thousands of hours as a physician, without compensation; I have gone from country to country for you, and often in your stead, when you yelled yourself hoarse with your I-ah, I-ah, allala! I was literally ready to die for you when, in the fight against the political plague, I drove you around in my car, with the death penalty hanging over my head; when I helped to protect your children against police raids when they walked in demonstration parades; when I spent all my money to establish mental health clinics where you could get counsel and help. But you only took from me, and never gave anything back. You only wanted to be saved, but in the course of 30 dreadful years of the emotional plague you did not have one fruitful thought. And when the second big war came to an end you found yourself exactly where you were before it broke out. Perhaps a little more to the "left" than the "right," *but not one millimeter FORWARD!* You gambled away the great French emancipation, and the even greater Russian emancipation you developed into the horror of the world. This terrible failure of yours which only great, lonesome hearts could understand without getting mad at you, without despising you, was followed by the despair of a whole world, that part of the world which was ready to sacrifice everything to you. In all the dreadful years, in a murderous half century, you uttered only platitudes and not a single healing, sensible word.

I did not lose heart, for in the meantime I had learned to understand your sickness still better and more deeply. I knew now that you could not possibly think or act other than you did. I recognized the deadly fear of the living in you, a fear which always makes you set out correctly and end wrongly. You don't understand that knowledge leads to *hope*. You only pump hope into yourself, not out of yourself. That's why, in the face of the complete disruption of your world, you call me an "optimist," Little Man. Yes, I am optimistic and full of the future. Why, you ask? I'll tell you:

As long as I clung to you, as you were and are, I was again and again hit in the face by your narrow-mindedness. Thousands of times I had forgotten what you had done to me when I had helped you, and thousands of times you reminded me of your sickness. Until I really opened my eyes and looked you full in the face. At first, I felt contempt and hatred come up in me. But gradually I learned to let my *understanding* of your sickness take effect against my hatred and my contempt. I was no longer angry at you for your dismal failure in your first attempt at mastery of the world. I began to understand that *this* was the way it had inevitably to happen, because for thousands of years you had been prevented from living life as it is.

I discovered the functional law of the living, Little Man, when you were going around yelling, "He is crazy!" At that time, you happened to be a little psychiatrist with a past in the youth movement and with a heart disease in the future, for you were impotent. Later on, you died of a broken heart, for one does not steal with impunity and does not defame someone without danger to life, if one has a mite of honesty in oneself. And you did have it in a corner of your soul, Little Man. When you turned from friend into enemy, you thought I was finished, and you tried to give me a final kick because you knew I was right and you were unable to follow. When, years later, I was back, like a Johnny-jump-up, this time stronger, clearer, more determined than ever, you were scared to death. And before dying, you realized that I had jumped over deep and wide chasms as well as over ditches you had dug in order

Until I really opened my eyes and looked you full in the face

to ruin me. Had you not proclaimed *my* teachings as *yours* in your cautious organization? I tell you: the honest people in the organization knew this; I know it because I have been told so. No, Little Man, tactics lead one only to a premature grave.

And since you are dangerous to life, since in your proximity one cannot stick to the truth without being stabbed in the back and without having dirt thrown into one's face, I have separated myself. I repeat: not from your future, but from your presence. Not from your humanity, but from your inhumanity and pettiness.

Only for *living life* am I still ready to make any sacrifice, but no longer for you, Little Man. Only a very short time ago I realized a gigantic error which I had entertained for some 25 years: I had devoted myself to you and your life because I believed *you* to be the living, the straightforward, the future and the hope. Like me, many other straightforward and true people hoped to find the living in you. Everyone of them perished. After finding this out, I decided not to perish under your narrow-mindedness and pettiness. For I have important things to do. *I have discovered the living,* Little Man. Now I no longer confuse you with the living which I felt in myself and sought in you.

Only if I clearly and sharply separate the living, its functions and characteristics, from your way of life, only then will I be able to make a real contribution to the security of the living and to *your* future. I know it takes courage to disavow you. But I can continue to work for the future because I do not pity you and because I do not have the urge to be made a little great person as do your miserable Führers.

For a short time now, the living has begun to rebel when it is being misused. This is the great beginning of your great future, and a dreadful end to all pettinesses of all little men. For in the meantime we have realized how the emotional plague works. It accuses Poland of intentions of military aggression just when it was decided to attack Poland. It accuses the rival of the intention of murder when it was just decided to murder him. It accuses healthy life of sexual swinishness just when some pornographic misdeed was hatched out.

One has gotten your number, Little Man; one has seen behind your façade of wretchedness and pitiableness. One wants you *to determine the course of the world,* with your *work* and your *achievement;* one does not want you to replace one tyrant by a worse

You are brutal behind your mask of sociality and friendliness

one. One begins to demand of you ever more strictly that you submit to the rules of life just as you ask it of others; that you improve yourself as you criticize others. One recognizes better and better your gossiping disposition, your greed, your freedom from responsibility, in brief, your general disease which smells up this beautiful world. I know you don't like to hear this, that you prefer to yell, Heil!, you bearer of the future of the proletariat or of the Fourth

Reich. But I believe you will succeed less than in the past. We have found the key to your secret of thousands of years. You are brutal behind your mask of sociality and friendliness, Little Man. You cannot spend half a day with me without giving yourself away. You don't believe me? Let me refresh your memory:

You remember the beautiful afternoon when, this time as a woodsman, you came to my cabin, looking for work? My puppy dog sniffed you and joyfully jumped up at you. You recognized him as the pup of a splendid hound. You said: "Why don't you put him on the chain, so he gets vicious? This dog is much too friendly." I said: "I don't want him to be a vicious dog on the chain. I don't like vicious dogs." My dear little woodsman, I have far more enemies in this world than you, but I still prefer the kindly dog who is friendly with everyone.

You remember the rainy Sunday when my restlessness about your biological rigidity drove me from my study to a bar? I sat at a table and had a whisky (no, Little Man, I am not a drinker, even though I like a drink from time to time). Well, I was having a highball. You had just come back from overseas, you were a little drunk, and I heard you describe the Japanese as "ugly apes." And then you said with that certain facial expression which I know so well from my therapeutic hours: "You know what ought to be done with those Japs out on the West Coast? Every one of them ought to be strung up, not quickly, but slowly, very slowly, another turn on the rope every five minutes, very slowly, this way . . . ." and you made the corresponding motion with your hand, Little Man. The waiter nodded his head approvingly and admired your heroic masculinity. Have you ever held a newborn Japanese baby in your arms, Little Patriot? No? For centuries to come, you will string up Japanese spies, American fliers, Russian peasant women, German officers, English anarchists and Greek Communists; you will shoot them, put them on the electric chair or into gas chambers; but nothing of all that will change the constipation of your guts or your mind, your incapacity for love, your rheumatism or your mental illness. No shooting or hanging will pull you out of your morass. Take a look at yourself, Little Man. It is your only hope.

You remember the day, Little Woman, when you sat in my study, brimming over with hatred for the man who had separated from you? For many years you had had him under your thumb, together with your mother and your aunts and grandnephews and cousins, until he began to shrink, for he had to take care of you and all your relatives. Finally, he pulled himself loose, in a last effort to maintain his feeling for life; and since he was not strong enough to gain his inner freedom from you, he came to me. He willingly paid your alimony, three quarters of his income, as required by law, as a penalty for his love for freedom. For he was a great artist, and art as well as genuine science does not tolerate shackles. But all you wanted was to be taken care of, by the man whom you hated bitterly, in spite of the fact that you had a profession of your own. You knew that I would help him to free himself from unjustified obligations. You got mad. You threatened me with the police, for, you said, *I* wanted to take all his money, taking advantage of his great need for help. In other words, you laid your bad intentions at my door, Poor Little Woman. But you never thought of improving yourself in your profession, for that would have meant to be independent, independent of the man whom for many years you had only hated. Do you believe that in this way you can build up a new world? You were acquainted with Socialists, I heard, who "knew all about me." Don't you see that you are a *type,* that there are millions like you who ruin this world? I know you are "weak" and "lonely," "tied to your mother's apron strings," and "helpless," you hate your hatred yourself, you can't stand yourself and are desperate. And that is why you ruin the life of your husband, Little Woman. And you swim in the stream of life as it generally is today. I also know that you have the Judges and District Attorneys on your side, for they have no answer to your misery.

I can still see you, little woman secretary in a Federal Court Building, as you put down my past and present, my opinions concerning possessions and Russia and democracy. I am asked for my social position. I say that I am an honorary member in three scientific and literary societies, among them the International Society for *Plasmogeny*. This seems to be impressive. Next time, an official says to me: "There is something queer here. It says you are an Honorary Member of the International Society for *Polygamy*. Is that correct?" And we both laugh about your little error, Little Phantastic Woman. Do you understand now why people say vile things about me? Because of *your* phantasy, and not because of my way of living. Is not all you remember of Rousseau that he wanted to go "back to nature," that he neglected his children and sent them to an orphanage? You are vicious, for you see and hear only that which is ugly and not that which is beautiful.

"Listen! I've seen him pull down his window-shades at one o'clock in the morning. What do you think he is doing? And during the day his shades are always up. Something must be wrong here!"

It will no longer help you to use such methods against the truth. We know them. You are not interested in my blinds, you are interested in hindering my truth. You want to continue to be the informer and defamer, to get your innocent neighbor in jail when you don't like his way of living, because he is kind, or free, because he works and does not pay any attention to you. You are very curious, Little Man, you snoop and defame. Aren't you protected by the fact that the police does not give away the identity of an informer?

"Listen, taxpapers! Here is a Professor of Philosophy. A great university in our city wants to employ him to teach the young. Down with him!"

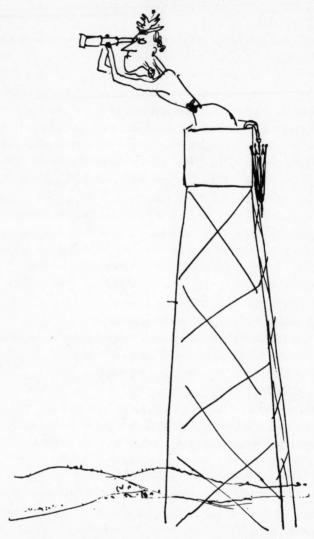

Leftist moralist checking up on orgone energy

And your upright housewife and taxpayer submits a petition against this teacher of the truth, and he does not get the position. You, upright tax-paying housewife, honorable bearer of patriots, were more powerful than 4000 years of natural philosophy. But one has begun to understand you, and sooner or later you will be put down.

"Listen, everybody interested in public morals! Around the corner lives a mother with her daughter. And the daughter receives her boy friend in the evening! Get her into court for keeping a bawdy house! Police! We want our morals protected!"

And this mother gets penalized because you, Little Man, snoop around other people's beds. You have shown yourself too clearly. We know your motive for "morals and order." Don't you try to pinch every waitress in the behind, moral Little Man? YES, WE WANT OUR SONS AND DAUGHTERS TO BE OPENLY HAPPY IN THEIR LOVE INSTEAD OF ENGAGING IN IT CLANDESTINELY, IN DARK ALLEYS AND ON DARK BACKSTAIRS. We want to respect the courageous and decent fathers and mothers who understand and protect the love of their adolescent sons and daughters. These fathers and mothers are the germ of the new generations of the future, with healthy bodies and healthy senses, without a trace of your filthy phantasy, Little Impotent Man of the 20th century.

"Listen to the newest one! A young man went to him for therapy and had to run with his pants down because he attacked him homosexually!"

Aren't you dribbling lasciviously at your mouth, Little Man, when you tell this "true story?" Do you know that it grew on *your* manure heap, from your constipation and your lasciviousness? I have never had homosexual longings, like you; I have never had the desire to seduce little girls, like you; I have never raped a woman, like you; I have never suffered from constipation, like you; I have never stolen love, like you, I have embraced women only when they wanted me and I wanted them; I have never exhibited myself publicly, as you do; I have no filthy phantasy like you, Little Man.

"Listen to this: he molested his secretary so that she had to run out of the house. He lived with her in one house, with the blinds down, and the lights were on until three o'clock in the morning!"

And he was a voluptuary who choked on pastry, you said about De La Mettrie; and he lives in a left-handed marriage, you said about crown prince Rudolf; and Mrs. Eleanor Roosevelt isn't quite all there, you said; and the President of X University has caught his wife with another man; and the teacher at this and that village school has a lover. Didn't you say these things, Little Man? You miserable citizen of this world, who for thousands of years has gambled his life away in that manner, and thus remains stuck in his morass!

"Catch him! He is a German spy, or maybe even a Russian, or an Icelandic one! I've seen him at three o'clock in the afternoon on 86th Street in New York, and with a woman, too!"

Do you know, Little Man, what a bedbug looks like in the Northern Lights? No? I didn't think so. One day, there will be strong laws against being a human bedbug, *strict laws for the protection of truth and love*. Just as today you put loving adolescents in the reform school, one day you will be put into an institution when you throw your dirt in decent people's faces. There will be a different kind of judges and state attorneys, who will not administer a formalistic sham-justice, but true justice and kindness. There will be *strict laws for the protection of life* which you will have to obey, no matter how much you will hate them. I know that for three or five or ten centuries you will continue to be a bearer of the emotional plague, of defamation, intrigue, diplomacy and inquisition. But in the end you will succumb to your own sense of cleanliness which now is so deeply buried in you as to be inaccessible.

I tell you, no Kaiser, no Tsar, no Father of all proletarians was able to conquer you. They only were able to enslave you, but none of them was able to rob you of your pettiness. *What is going to conquer you is your sense of cleanliness, your longing for life.* There is no doubt about that, Little Man. Cleansed of your smallness and pettiness, you will begin to *think*. True, this thinking, at first, will be pitiful, erroneous and aimless; but you will begin to think seriously. You will have to learn to bear the pain which your thinking will bring with itself, just as I and others had to bear the pain of the thinking *about you;* for years, silently, with clenched teeth. This pain of ours will make you think. Once you have started to think you will not cease to marvel at your last 4000 years of "civilization." You will be unable to understand how it was possible that your newspapers wrote about nothing but parading, decorating, shootings, hangings, diplomacy, chicanery, mobilizations, demobilizations and again mobilizations, pacts, drilling and bombing, and that all this did not make you see red. You might have understood yourself if you had done nothing but eat up all that stuff with sheeplike patience. But what you won't be able to take for a long time is the fact that through centuries you aped and parrotted all this stuff, that you thought your correct thoughts about it all were wrong, and thought your wrong ideas about it were patriotic. You will be ashamed of your history, and this is our only hope that our great-grandchildren will be saved from reading your military history. It will no longer be possible for you to stage a great revolution only to go back to some "Peter the Great."

A GLANCE IN THE FUTURE. I cannot tell you what your future will look like. I cannot know whether you will reach the moon or Mars with the cosmic orgone I discovered. Nor can I know how your space ships will fly or land; or whether you will use sunlight to light your houses at night. But I can tell you what you are NO LONGER going to do, 500 or 1000 or 5000 years hence.

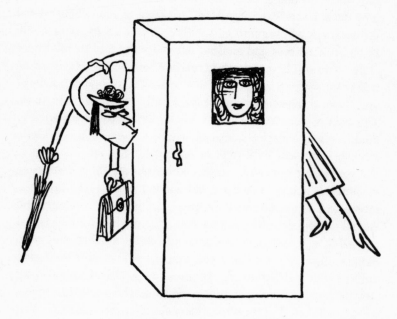

Orgastic Potency? Presumably

"Listen to the visionary! He can tell me what I am not going to do! Is he a dictator?"

I am not a dictator, Little Man, although your pettiness would have made it easy for me to become one. Your dictators can only tell you what you *cannot* do in the present without being sent to the gas chamber. But they cannot tell you what you are going to do in the far future, no more than they can make a tree grow faster.

"And where do *you* get your wisdom, intellectual servant of the revolutionary proletariat?"

From your own depth, you eternal proletarian of human reason.

"Listen to that! He gets his wisdom from my own depth! I haven't any depth. And what kind of an individualistic word is that, 'depth'!"

Yes, Little Man, you have depth in yourself, you only don't know it. You are deadly afraid of your depth, that's why you don't feel it or see it. That's why you get dizzy when you look into the depth and totter as if at the verge of an abyss. You are afraid of falling and of losing your "individuality" when you should let yourself go. With the best intentions to reach yourself, you arrive always at the same: the little, cruel, envious, greedy, thievish man. If you were not deep in your depth, Little Man, I would not have written this talk to you. I know this depth in you, for I have discovered it when you came to me as a physician with your worries. This depth in you is your great future. That's why I can tell you what you certainly are no longer going to do in the future, because you will be unable to comprehend how it was possible that in the era of un-culture of 4000 years you did all the things that you did. Do you want to listen now?

"All right. Why shouldn't I listen to a nice little Utopia? There is nothing that can be done, my good doctor. I am, and I am going to remain, the poor little man of the street, who has no opinion of his own. Who am I anyhow to . . ."

Listen. You hide behind the legend of the Little Man because you are afraid of being picked up by the stream of life and *having to* swim, if for no other reason, for the sake of your children and their children.

The first of all the things that you are no longer going to do is to feel yourself to be the little man who has no opinion of his own and who says, "Who am I anyhow . . ." You *do have* your own opinion, and in the future you will consider it a great shame *not* to know it, *not* to advocate it and *not* to express it.

"But what will public opinion say about my opinion? I am going to be squashed like a worm if I express my own opinion!"

What you call "public opinion," Little Man, is the sum total of all the opinions of all little men and women. Every little man and every little woman has a correct opinion and a wrong opinion. The wrong opinions they have because they are afraid of the wrong opinions of other little men and women. This is why the correct opinions don't come out. For example, you will no longer believe that you "don't count." You will know and advocate your knowledge that you are the bearer of human society. Don't run away. Don't be so afraid. It is not so terrible to be the responsible bearer of human society.

"What do I have to do to be the bearer of human society?"

You don't have to do anything special or new. All you have to do is to continue what you are doing: plowing your fields, wield your hammer, examine your patients, take your children to school or to the playground, report on the events of the day, penetrate ever more deeply into the secrets of nature. All these things you do already. But you think that all this is unimportant, and that what is important is only what Marshal Decoratus or Prince Inflatus, the Knight in shining armor, are doing.

"But you are a visionary, doctor! Don't you see that Marshal Decoratus and Prince Inflatus have the soldiers and the weapons to make war, to draft me for war service, to shoot my field, my laboratory or my study to pieces?"

You are drafted for war service, and your field and your factory are shot to pieces because you yell, Heil, when you are drafted and your factories are shot to pieces. Prince Inflatus, the Knight in shining armor, would have no soldiers and no arms if you clearly knew, and stood up for your knowledge, that a field has to yield wheat and a factory furniture or shoes, and not arms, and that fields and factories are not there in order to be ruined. All this your Marshal Decoratus and your Prince Inflatus do not know, for they never worked themselves in the field, the factory or the laboratory; they believe that your work is done for the honor of the German or the proletarian fatherland, and not in order to feed and clothe your children.

"What should I do, then? I hate war, my wife cries miserably when I'm drafted, my children starve when the proletarian armies occupy my land, and the corpses pile up by the million. All I want is to work my fields, and after work to play with my children and to love my wife, and on Sundays I want to make music and dance and sing. What am I to do?"

All you have to do is to continue what you have always done and always want to do: to do your work, to let your children grow up happily, to love your wife. IF YOU DID THIS CLEARLY AND UN-FLINCHINGLY THERE WOULD BE NO WAR which puts your wife at the mercy of the sexually starved soldiers of the fatherland of all proletarians, which makes your orphaned children starve in the street, which makes you stare with glassy eyes at the sky on some far "field of glory."

"But what am I to do if I want to live for my work and my wife and my children, and then the Huns or the Germans or the Japanese or the Russians or whoever forces war on me? Must I not defend my home?"

You are right, Little Man. When the Hun of this or that nation attacks you you will have to grab your rifle. But what you don't see is that the "Huns" of all nations are nothing but millions of other little men who keep yelling, Heil! when Prince Inflatus, who does not work, calls them to the colors; that they, like you, believe that they don't count and say, "Who am I to have an opinion of my own?"

Who am I to have an opinion of my own?

Once you know that you *are* somebody, that you *have* a correct opinion of your own, and that your field and your factory have to serve *life* and not death, then you will be able to answer your question for yourself. You will not need any diplomats for that. Instead of going on yelling, Heil, and decorating the tomb of the "Unknown Soldier," instead of letting your Prince Inflatus or your Marshal of all proletarians trample your national consciousness, you should oppose them with your *self-confidence* and your *work consciousness*. (I know your "Unknown Soldier" well, Little Man. I got to know him when I fought in the Italian mountains. He is the same little man as you, who believed not to have an opinion of his own and who said, "Who am I, anyhow . . ."). You could get to know your brother, the little man in Japan, in China, in any Hun country and could let him know your correct opinion of your job as a worker, physician, farmer, father or husband, and could convince him finally that all he has to do to make any war impossible is to adhere to his work and his love.

"Well and good. But now they have these atom bombs, and one of them is enough to kill hundreds of thousands of people!"

You still don't think straight, Little Man. Do you believe that Prince Inflatus, the Knight in shining armor, builds your atom bombs? No, it is again only little men who yell, Heil!, instead of ceasing to make atom bombs. You see, it always comes back to one and the same thing, to you, Little Man, and your own thinking, correct or false. If you were not such a microscopically small man, you greatest scientist of the 20th century, you would have developed a world consciousness instead of a national consciousness and would have found the means of *preventing* the atom bomb from breaking into this world; or, if that had been impossible, you would have exercised your influence, in unmistakable words, to put it out of function. You turn around in a maze of your own invention, and you don't find your way out because you look the wrong way and think the wrong way. But you promised to all the little men that your atomic energy was going to cure their cancer and their rheumatism when you knew perfectly well that this would never be possible, that you had created a murderous weapon and nothing but that. With that, you have landed in the same blind alley in which your physics has landed. *You are finished, forever.* You know, Little Man, that I have presented you with the therapeutic possibilities of *my* cosmic energy. But you keep silent about it, and continue to die of cancer and a broken heart, and, dying, you still yell, "Heil, long live culture and technic!" But I tell you, Little Man: you have dug your own grave with open eyes. You believe that a new era has arrived, the "era of atomic energy." It has arrived, but not in the way you think. Not in your inferno, but in my quiet, industrious laboratory in a far corner of America.

It is entirely up to you, Little Man, whether or not you have to go to war. If you only knew that you are working for life and not for death. If you only knew that all little men on this earth are exactly like you, in their good and their bad traits.

Sooner or later — it all depends on you — you will no longer yell, Heil, and will no longer work your fields for the destruction of your wheat, or your factory as a target of guns. Sooner or later you will no longer be willing to work for death but only for life.

"Should I call a general strike?"

I don't know whether you should do that or something else. Your general strike is a bad means, because with it you expose yourself to the justified reproach that you let your own women and children starve. In striking, you do not prove your great responsibility for the weal and woe of your society. When you strike you do *not* work. But one day you will WORK for your life, not strike. Call it a work strike, if you wish to stick to the word "strike." But strike by working, for yourself, your children, your wife or your girl, your society, your product or your farm. Tell them that you have no time for their war, that you have more important things to do. Put a fence around a large plot outside each city of the earth, and there let the diplomats and marshals kill one another personally. This, Little Man, would be the thing to do if you were no longer yelling, Heil, and no longer believed that you are nobody and have no opinion of your own.

Everything is in your hand, your life and that of your children, your hammer and your stethoscope. I know you shake your head, you think I am an Utopian, or maybe even a "Red." You ask when your life will be good and secure, Little Man. The answer is alien to your way of being:

Your life will be good and secure when aliveness will mean more to you than security; love more than money; your freedom more than party line or public opinion; when the mood of Beethoven or Bach will be the mood of your total existence (you have it in you, Little Man, buried deeply in a corner of your existence); when your thinking will be in harmony, and no longer at variance, with your feelings; when you will be able to comprehend your gifts in *time* and to recognize your aging in time; when you will live the thoughts of great men instead of the misdeeds of great warriors; when the teachers of your children will be better paid than the politicians; when you will have more respect for the love between man and woman than for a marriage license; when you will recognize your errors in thinking in time, and not too late, as today; when you will feel elevation in hearing truths, and feel horror of formalities; when you will have intercourse with your work comrades directly, and not through diplomats; when your adolescent daughter's happiness in love will delight instead of enraging you; when you will only shake your head at the times when one punished little children for touching their love organs; when human faces on the street will express freedom, animation and joy and no longer sadness and misery; when people no longer will walk on this earth with retracted and rigid pelves and deadened sexual organs.

You want guidance and advice, Little Man. You have had guidance and advice, good and bad, through thousands of years. It is not because of poor advice that you are still in your misery, but because of your pettiness. I could give you good advice, but, as you think and are, you would not be capable of putting it into action in the interest of all.

Suppose I advised you to stop all diplomacy, and to replace it with your professional and personal brotherliness with all shoemakers, carpenters, machinists, technicians, physicians, educators, writers, administrators, miners or farmers of all countries; to let all shoemakers of the world decide the best way of providing shoes to all Chinese children; to let all miners find out by themselves how people can be kept from freezing, to let the educators of all countries and nations find out how all newborn children are to be guarded against later impotence and mental disease, etc. What would you do, Little Man, confronted with these matter-of-course things of human life?

You would certainly tell me, yourself or through some representative of your party, church, government or union (unless you jailed me immediately as a "Red"):

"Who am I to replace international diplomatic intercourse by the international intercourse of work and social achievement?"

Or: "We cannot eliminate the national differences in the development of economy and culture."

Or: "Do you want us to have truck with the Fascist Germans, or Japanese, and with the Communist Russians, and with the capitalist Americans?"

Or: "I am interested, first of all, in my Russian, German, American, English, Jewish or Arabic fatherland."

Or: "I have plenty to do getting my own life in order and to get along with my tailors' union. Let somebody else take care of the tailors of other nations."

Or: "Don't listen to this capitalist, Bolshevik, Fascist, Trotzkyite, Internationalist, Sexualist, Jew, Foreigner, Intellectual, Dreamer, Utopian, Demagogue, Crazy Man, Individualist, and Anarchist. Don't you have any American, Russian, German, English, Jewish consciousness?"

Am I nothing at all?

You can be dead sure that you would use one of these slogans, or others, to get around your responsibility for human intercourse.

"Am I nothing at all? You don't acknowledge one decent trait in me! After all, I work hard, provide for my wife and my children, I lead a decent life and serve my country. I can't be as bad as all that!"

I know you are a decent, solid, industrious being, like a bee or an ant. All I did was to disclose the little man in you who ruins your life, and has done so for thousands of years. You are GREAT, Little Man, when you are not small and petty. Your greatness, Little Man, is the only hope left. You are great when you carry on your trade lovingly, when you enjoy carving and building and painting and decorating and sowing, when you enjoy the blue sky and the deer and the dew and music and dancing, your growing children and the beautiful body of your woman or your man; when you go to the planetarium to learn to understand your sky, or to the library to read what other men and women think about life. You are great when, as a grandfather, you hold your grandchild on your knees and tell him about times long past, when you look into an uncertain future with his trusting childlike curiosity. You are great, as a mother, when you lull your newborn to sleep, when, with tears in your eyes, you hope, out of your full heart, for his future happiness, when, every hour through the years, you build this future in him.

You are great, Little Man, when you sing the good old folk songs, or when you dance to the tune of an accordion, for the folk songs are warm and soothing, and are the same all over the world. And you are great when you say to your friend:

"I thank my good fate that it was given to me to live my life free from filth and greed, to experience the growth of my children, their first babbling, reaching, walking, playing, asking questions, laughing and loving; that I kept my full feeling for the spring and its mild winds, for the bubbling of the brook past the house and the song of the birds in the woods; that I did not take part in the gossip of vicious neighbors; that I was happy in the embrace of my mate and was able to feel the streaming of life in my body; that in confused times I did not lose my sense of direction, and that my life had a meaning. For I have always listened to the voice in myself which said: 'There is only one thing that counts: to live one's life well and happily. Follow the voice of your heart, even if it leads you off the path of timid souls. Do not become hard and embittered, even if life tortures you at times.' And in the quiet of the evening, the day's work done, when I sit on the meadow in front of the house with my wife or my child and feel the breathing of nature, I hear a melody, the melody of the future: 'Oh ye millions, I embrace ye, With a kiss for all the world!' Then I wish fervently that this life would learn to insist on its rights, to change the hard and the timid souls who make the cannons sound. They only do it because life eluded them. And I hug my little son who asks me: 'Father, the sun has gone down. Where has it gone? Will it come back soon?' And I tell him: 'Yes, son, it will be back soon to warm us.'"

———————————

I have arrived at the conclusion of my talk to you, Little Man. There is ever so much more that I could tell you. But if you have read this talk attentively and honestly, you will discover yourself as the Little Man even in the places which I have not shown you. For it is always the same quality which pervades all your petty actions and thoughts.

Whatever you have done to me or will do to me in the future, whether you glorify me as a genius or put me in a mental institution, whether you adore me as your savior or hang me as a spy, sooner or later necessity will force you to comprehend that *I have discovered the laws of the living* and handed you the tool with which to govern your life, with a conscious goal, as heretofore you were able only to govern machines. I have been a faithful engineer of your organism. Your grandchildren will follow in my footsteps and will be good engineers of human nature. I have disclosed to you the infinitely vast field of the living in you, of your cosmic nature. That is my great reward.

The dictators and tyrants, the sly-boots and the venomous, the dungbeetles and the coyotes will suffer what an old sage once predicted:

> I planted the seed of holy words
> in this world.
> When long since the palmtree will have died,
> the rock decayed;
> When long since the shining monarchs
> have been blown away like rotted leaves:
> Through every deluge a thousand arks
> will carry my word:
> It will prevail!